Goal-Scoring Artistry: Skill Development and Technique for Deadly Shooting and Finishing in Soccer

Written by Aldin Beslagic

Table of Contents

Chapter 4: Power and Long-Range Shooting
- Generating power through proper technique and body mechanics
- Exercises to develop leg strength and explosive shooting
- Techniques for shooting from distance and outside the box
- Shooting with power while maintaining accuracy

Chapter 5: Finishing in Various Game Situations
- Techniques for finishing one-on-one with the goalkeeper
- Understanding different angles and positions for finishing
- Shooting under pressure from tight spaces and crowded defenses
- Capitalizing on rebounds and loose balls

Chapter 6: Goal-Scoring Movement and Positioning
- Creating space and making intelligent runs to get into goal-scoring positions
- Timing runs to stay onside and exploit defensive vulnerabilities
- Analyzing goal-scoring movements of top strikers
- Improving anticipation and decision-making in the final third

Chapter 7: Developing a Deadly Instinct in the Box
- Reading the game and anticipating scoring opportunities

- Improving reaction time and instinctive finishing
- Positioning in the box for tap-ins, headers, and poacher goals
- Training drills to enhance predatory instincts

Chapter 8: Mental Strategies for Overcoming Goalkeeper Challenges
- Analyzing goalkeepers' weaknesses and exploiting them
- Techniques for outsmarting goalkeepers during one-on-one situations
- Penalty-taking strategies for high success rates
- Maintaining composure in front of the goal

Chapter 9: Training Regimens for Goal-Scorers
- Tailoring practice sessions to improve shooting and finishing skills
- Incorporating individual and team drills into training routines
- Physical conditioning for explosive shooting and sustained performance
- Assessing progress and tracking improvement over time

Conclusion:
- Recap of key points discussed throughout the book
- Encouragement to continue honing goal-scoring skills through dedicated practice
- Inspiring anecdotes and quotes from successful goal-scorers

- Final thoughts on the artistry and joy of scoring goals in soccer

About The Author – Aldin Beslagic

As an author, soccer coach, and former Division 1 player, my life has been passionately intertwined with the beautiful game of football. With a solid foundation in finance and international business, as well as a Master's in Accounting and Business Administration from Quinnipiac University, I have honed my leadership and interpersonal skills, which have proven invaluable in my coaching journey.

My extensive playing experience, including captaining the Quinnipiac University soccer team during my senior year, has instilled in me a deep understanding of football techniques and tactics. This knowledge, combined with my innate ability to maintain positive and professional relationships with athletes, has been instrumental in shaping my coaching style.

Throughout my coaching career, I have been dedicated to fostering a positive and empowering environment for athletes. As the founder of PassionateSoccerCoach.com, a leading online platform for soccer enthusiasts, players, and coaches, I have immersed myself in developing comprehensive resources to support the growth and advancement of the sport. From curating high-quality training drills to providing tactical analyses, coaching tips, and motivational strategies, I take pride in equipping fellow coaches and players with the tools they need to succeed.

In addition to my involvement with PassionateSoccerCoach.com, I have held pivotal roles as the Head Coach for the Connecticut Football Club, where I have overseen game scheduling, managed group travel, and provided guidance on the development aspect, team and individual growth, and soccer aspiration. As the Director of Coaching, I directed a competitive youth soccer club, handling various aspects from budgeting and tournaments to coaching education and player development.

My dedication to continuous improvement is evident through the licenses I hold, including a National D License from U.S.S.F., CJSA Coaching Licenses, and CPR certification. Having played for the prestigious TSV Guglingen German Youth Team during my early years, I understand the transformative power of soccer on and off the field.

Through my writing, coaching, and leadership experiences, I strive to elevate the standards of soccer coaching, foster a love for the sport, and inspire players to reach their fullest potential. My journey as an author reflects a deep passion for sharing knowledge and insights, allowing me to leave a positive impact on the soccer community and the lives of those I coach.

Introduction:

Importance of scoring goals in soccer and its impact on team success

Scoring goals is the ultimate objective in soccer, as it directly determines the outcome of matches and greatly influences a team's success. A well-executed goal not only ignites the passion of players and fans but also serves as a catalyst for momentum and confidence within the team. In this chapter, we will explore the significance of goal-scoring in soccer and delve into its profound impact on team performance and success.

1. The Essence of Goal-Scoring:
Goals are the lifeblood of soccer, representing the culmination of teamwork, skill, strategy, and sheer determination. They are the tangible reward for players' efforts and signify the effectiveness of their attacking play. Scoring goals is not only thrilling for the team and its supporters but also a reflection of its ability to dominate matches and impose its style of play on opponents.

2. Psychological Boost:
The act of scoring a goal has a profound psychological impact on both individuals and the collective team. It injects a surge of confidence, motivation, and belief, uplifting players' spirits and driving them to perform at their best. A single goal can completely alter the momentum of a match, shifting the

balance of power and boosting the attacking team's morale while simultaneously deflating the opposition.

3.   Offensive Pressure and Defensive Freedom:
Teams that possess potent goal-scoring capabilities place tremendous pressure on their opponents' defenses. The fear of conceding goals forces the opposition to adopt more conservative tactics, opening up spaces in the defensive structure. This provides opportunities for the attacking team to exploit, creating gaps and generating scoring chances.
Conversely, strong offensive capabilities grant defensive stability and freedom to the team. When a team is proficient at scoring goals, opponents are compelled to devote more resources to their defensive duties, limiting their attacking options. This eases the defensive burden on the team, allowing them to focus on thwarting the opposition's attacks and maintaining control of the game.

4.   Boosting Team Morale and Unity:
Scoring goals not only impacts individual players but also strengthens the collective bond within the team. It fosters a sense of camaraderie, shared success, and trust among teammates. Celebrating a goal together builds a cohesive team spirit and a shared sense of purpose, forging a strong connection on and off the field.

5.   Enhancing Spectator Experience:
Goals are the pinnacle of excitement for soccer fans worldwide. They create moments of jubilation, elation, and celebration that leave lasting memories. The ability to score goals consistently not only entertains the fans but also helps

to build a loyal and passionate supporter base. This, in turn, generates financial and commercial benefits for the team, contributing to its long-term success.

6. Influencing Game Dynamics and Tactics:
The act of scoring a goal influences the flow and dynamics of the game. When a team takes the lead, it can dictate the tempo, control possession, and force the opposition to chase the game. Scoring goals can also disrupt the opponent's tactical plans, compelling them to alter their approach and take more risks, which opens up further opportunities for the attacking team.

7. Achieving Victory:
Ultimately, the goal of any soccer team is to win matches. Goals are the primary means of accomplishing this objective. Teams that possess efficient goal-scoring abilities significantly increase their chances of securing victories. By consistently converting scoring opportunities into goals, a team can build a successful season, climb the league standings, and contend for titles.

Scoring goals in soccer holds immense significance for individual players, teams, and their supporters. It serves as a driving force that impacts team morale, tactical considerations, and overall success. A team's ability to score goals consistently is a testament to its attacking prowess, skill development, and strategic approach. By understanding and appreciating the importance of goal-scoring, players and teams can focus their efforts on mastering the art of deadly shooting and finishing, setting themselves up for greater achievements and memorable moments on the soccer field.

Overview of the book's objective: to provide comprehensive guidance on skill development and technique for effective shooting and finishing

"Goal-Scoring Artistry: Skill Development and Technique for Deadly Shooting and Finishing in Soccer" aims to provide readers with a comprehensive guide to enhance their skill development and technique in shooting and finishing. This book serves as a valuable resource for players, coaches, and enthusiasts who are passionate about improving their goal-scoring abilities.

By focusing specifically on shooting and finishing, the book delves deep into the intricacies of these critical aspects of the game. It goes beyond the basics, offering a detailed exploration of the techniques, strategies, and mindset required to become a lethal goal-scorer.

The book's objective can be summarized as follows:

1. Technical Proficiency: The book emphasizes the importance of technical proficiency in shooting and finishing. It provides step-by-step instructions, illustrations, and expert insights to help readers refine their shooting techniques, such as body positioning, balance, and striking the ball cleanly. It also covers a range of shooting techniques, including laces, instep,

volleys, and chips, ensuring readers have a varied arsenal of skills to call upon.

2. Precision and Accuracy: Effective finishing requires precision and accuracy. The book offers detailed guidance on developing the ability to place shots in various areas of the goal, allowing readers to maximize their chances of scoring. It includes exercises, drills, and tips to enhance accuracy, ensuring that shots find their intended target with consistency.

3. Power and Long-Range Shooting: While accuracy is crucial, the book recognizes the significance of power in goal-scoring. It provides insights and training regimens to develop leg strength, generate power, and unleash long-range shots. By mastering the techniques for shooting with power while maintaining accuracy, readers can become more dynamic and unpredictable goal-scorers.

4. Game Situations and Movement: Goal-scoring opportunities arise in a variety of game situations. The book offers guidance on finishing one-on-one with the goalkeeper, exploiting different angles and positions, and shooting under pressure from tight spaces and crowded defenses. It also delves into the importance of intelligent movement and positioning to create scoring opportunities and capitalize on them effectively.

5. Mental Preparedness: The book recognizes the psychological aspect of goal-scoring and emphasizes

the development of a goal-scorer's mindset. It explores techniques to enhance confidence, focus, and mental resilience, enabling readers to perform at their best in high-pressure situations. It also provides strategies for overcoming goalkeeper challenges and maintaining composure in front of the goal.

6. Training Regimens: To achieve proficiency in shooting and finishing, dedicated training is essential. The book outlines comprehensive training regimens tailored specifically for goal-scoring skill development. It includes individual and team drills, physical conditioning exercises, and methods to assess progress and track improvement over time.

By encompassing these key elements, "Goal-Scoring Artistry" aims to equip readers with the necessary knowledge and skills to elevate their goal-scoring abilities. Whether readers are aspiring strikers, seasoned players looking to enhance their proficiency, or coaches seeking to develop their players' skills, this book serves as a valuable guide to unlock the artistry of deadly shooting and finishing in soccer.

Chapter 1: The Mindset of a Goal-Scorer

Understanding the psychology behind goal-scoring

The ability to score goals in soccer extends beyond technical skill and physical attributes. Understanding the psychology behind goal-scoring is crucial for players to perform at their best and consistently find the back of the net. This chapter delves into the psychological aspects that influence goal-scoring and provides insights to help players develop a winning mindset.

1. Confidence: The Foundation of Goal-Scoring
   - Exploring the relationship between confidence and goal-scoring success
   - Strategies to build and maintain confidence on and off the field
   - Overcoming self-doubt and developing a positive mindset

2. Visualization: Creating Success in the Mind
   - Harnessing the power of mental imagery to enhance goal-scoring abilities
   - Techniques for visualizing successful shots and finishes
   - Utilizing visualization as a tool for preparation and performance enhancement

3. Goal-Setting: Setting the Stage for Achievement
   - The importance of setting specific, measurable, and attainable goals
   - Short-term and long-term goal-setting strategies for goal-scoring success
   - Tracking progress and adjusting goals as needed

4. Focus and Concentration: Blocking Out Distractions
   - Developing mental focus to maintain concentration during crucial moments
   - Techniques for staying in the present moment and avoiding distractions
   - Enhancing mental resilience to overcome setbacks and stay focused on scoring goals

5. Dealing with Pressure: Thriving in High-Stakes Situations
   - Understanding the impact of pressure on goal-scoring performance
   - Strategies to manage nerves and perform under pressure
   - Practicing mental routines to maintain composure during important matches

6. Learning from Failure: Bouncing Back Stronger
   - Embracing failure as a learning opportunity and not allowing it to deter goal-scoring confidence
   - Techniques for analyzing mistakes and using them to improve future performances
   - Developing a resilient mindset to bounce back from missed chances or unsuccessful games

7. Positive Self-Talk: Shaping the Inner Dialogue
   • The power of positive self-talk in boosting confidence and motivation
   • Techniques for replacing negative thoughts with positive affirmations
   • Building a strong self-belief system to fuel goal-scoring success
   •

8. Emotional Intelligence: Channeling Emotions for Performance
   • Understanding and managing emotions that can impact goal-scoring performance
   • Techniques for channeling emotions in a productive manner on the field
   • Developing emotional intelligence to stay composed and focused during high-pressure situations

The psychology behind goal-scoring in soccer plays a vital role in a player's ability to perform at their best and consistently score goals. By understanding and mastering the psychological aspects discussed in this chapter, players can develop the mental resilience, confidence, focus, and motivation needed to become deadly goal-scorers. Incorporating these psychological strategies alongside technical skills and physical abilities will help players unlock their full potential and achieve success on the field.

Developing confidence, focus, and mental resilience

Confidence, focus, and mental resilience are key psychological attributes that contribute to goal-scoring success in soccer. This chapter explores strategies and techniques to develop these qualities, enabling players to perform at their best even in challenging situations.

1. Building Confidence:
   - Recognizing the importance of confidence in goal-scoring
   - Identifying individual strengths and areas for improvement
   - Setting realistic goals to boost confidence gradually
   - Utilizing positive self-talk and affirmations
   - Celebrating successes and learning from failures

2. Enhancing Focus:
   - Understanding the role of focus in maintaining concentration during matches
   - Practicing mindfulness techniques to improve focus and awareness
   - Developing pre-game and pre-shot routines to establish focus
   - Utilizing visualization exercises to enhance focus on scoring opportunities

3. Cultivating Mental Resilience:
   - Embracing challenges and setbacks as opportunities for growth

- Developing a growth mindset that focuses on continuous improvement
- Managing stress and pressure through relaxation techniques
- Utilizing positive visualization and mental rehearsal to bounce back from failures
- Seeking support from coaches, teammates, and mental performance professionals

4. Overcoming Negative Thoughts and Self-Doubt:
   - Recognizing and challenging negative thoughts and self-doubt patterns
   - Replacing negative thoughts with positive affirmations and self-talk
   - Developing strategies to stay present and focused during matches
   - Reframing failures and setbacks as learning experiences
   - Using past successes as a source of motivation and confidence

5. Goal-Setting for Confidence and Focus:
   - Setting specific and achievable goals related to confidence and focus
   - Breaking down long-term goals into smaller, manageable steps
   - Establishing a system to track progress and celebrate milestones
   - Adjusting goals as needed to maintain motivation and challenge oneself

6. Mental Preparation for High-Pressure Situations:
   - Practicing mental imagery and visualization for challenging scenarios
   - Simulating pressure situations in training to build resilience
   - Utilizing deep breathing and relaxation techniques to manage nerves
   - Developing coping strategies for dealing with stress during matches
   - Incorporating mindfulness exercises to stay focused during critical moments

7. Learning from Successful Role Models:
   - Studying and analyzing successful goal-scorers' mindset and approach
   - Identifying key mental attributes displayed by accomplished players
   - Adopting effective mental strategies used by role models
   - Drawing inspiration and motivation from their achievements

Confidence, focus, and mental resilience are crucial psychological attributes that enable players to excel in goal-scoring. By implementing the strategies and techniques discussed in this chapter, players can develop and strengthen these qualities, allowing them to perform at their best consistently. Cultivating confidence, honing focus, and building mental resilience will enhance players' overall goal-scoring abilities and contribute to their success on the soccer field.

Visualization and goal-setting techniques

Visualization and goal-setting are powerful tools that can significantly enhance goal-scoring abilities in soccer. This chapter explores the techniques and strategies involved in effectively utilizing visualization and goal-setting to maximize performance and achieve desired outcomes.

1. The Power of Visualization:
    *   Understanding the concept of visualization and its impact on goal-scoring success
    *   Exploring the science behind how visualization affects the brain and body
    *   Techniques for creating vivid mental imagery of successful goal-scoring scenarios
    *   Incorporating multisensory details to enhance the effectiveness of visualization

2. Setting Clear and Specific Goals:
    *   Recognizing the importance of goal-setting in goal-scoring development
    *   Establishing clear, specific, and measurable goals for individual and team performance
    *   Breaking down long-term goals into short-term, attainable objectives
    *   Utilizing the SMART (Specific, Measurable, Achievable, Relevant, Time-bound) framework for effective goal-setting

3. Long-Term Goal-Setting:
   - Setting ambitious but realistic long-term goals for personal growth and development
   - Identifying areas of improvement to focus on in goal-scoring abilities
   - Planning and organizing training regimens and skill development programs
   - Establishing benchmarks and milestones to track progress toward long-term goals

4. Short-Term Goal-Setting:
   - Establishing short-term goals that are aligned with long-term objectives
   - Breaking down larger goals into manageable steps and tasks
   - Prioritizing goals based on individual needs and skill development areas
   - Creating a timeline and action plan for achieving short-term goals

5. Monitoring Progress and Adjusting Goals:
   - Implementing systems to track progress and measure goal attainment
   - Regularly assessing performance and identifying areas for improvement
   - Adjusting goals as necessary to adapt to changing circumstances or aspirations
   - Seeking feedback from coaches, teammates, and mentors to evaluate progress

6. Mental Rehearsal and Pre-Game Visualization:
   - Incorporating mental rehearsal techniques to mentally prepare for matches
   - Visualizing the entire goal-scoring process, from positioning to execution
   - Practicing pre-game visualization routines to enhance confidence and focus
   - Using visualization to simulate challenging situations and develop effective strategies

7. Creating a Goal-Oriented Mindset:
   - Developing a positive and proactive mindset focused on achieving goals
   - Cultivating self-belief and optimism in the pursuit of goal-scoring success
   - Overcoming obstacles and setbacks through resilience and determination
   - Using goals as sources of motivation, inspiration, and accountability

8. Goal-Setting as a Team:
   - Aligning individual goals with the team's overall objectives
   - Establishing collective goals for offensive performance and goal-scoring success
   - Fostering a supportive and collaborative environment to achieve team goals
   - Celebrating and acknowledging goal-scoring achievements as a collective unit

Visualization and goal-setting techniques are invaluable tools for enhancing goal-scoring abilities in soccer. By mastering the art of mental imagery and setting clear, measurable goals, players can tap into their full potential and achieve remarkable results. Incorporating these techniques into training routines and match preparations empowers players to develop focus, motivation, and a strategic mindset. Ultimately, visualization and goal-setting become integral parts of a player's journey toward becoming a lethal goal-scorer and contributing to the success of their team.

Chapter 2: Essential Technical Skills for Shooting

Perfecting the shooting technique: body positioning, balance, and striking the ball cleanly

The shooting technique is a fundamental aspect of goal-scoring in soccer. This chapter focuses on the key elements of body positioning, balance, and striking the ball cleanly. By mastering these components, players can improve the accuracy, power, and consistency of their shots, increasing their chances of finding the back of the net.

1. Understanding Body Positioning:
    - The role of body positioning in creating shooting opportunities
    - Optimizing body alignment to generate power and accuracy
    - Positioning the non-kicking foot for stability and control
    - Adjusting body position based on the type of shot and shooting scenario

2. Achieving Balance and Stability:
    - The importance of balance in executing successful shots
    - Techniques for maintaining balance during the shooting motion
    - Utilizing the arms for balance and counterbalancing the body

- Developing core strength and stability for improved shooting technique

3. Striking the Ball Cleanly:
   - The significance of striking the ball cleanly for accuracy and power
   - Proper foot placement and contact with the ball
   - Generating a clean follow-through for improved shot quality
   - Techniques for consistent ball contact and avoiding mishits

4. Footwork and Approach:
   - The role of footwork in setting up the shooting technique
   - Techniques for quick and efficient footwork to create shooting opportunities
   - Incorporating changes of pace and direction to deceive defenders and gain shooting space
   - Coordinating footwork with body positioning and balance for optimal shot execution

5. Developing Technique through Repetition:
   - The importance of repetitive practice in perfecting shooting technique
   - Incorporating shooting drills and exercises into training sessions
   - Using progressive drills to gradually increase difficulty and challenge players
   - Analyzing and adjusting technique based on feedback and self-assessment

6. Shot Selection and Decision-Making:
    *   Understanding shot selection based on game situations and goal-scoring opportunities
    *   Assessing shooting angles and distances to make informed decisions
    *   Developing the ability to make split-second decisions under pressure
    *   Practicing shooting scenarios to improve decision-making and shot accuracy

7. Video Analysis and Feedback:
    *   Utilizing video analysis to assess shooting technique and identify areas for improvement
    *   Seeking feedback from coaches, trainers, and teammates to refine shooting technique
    *   Incorporating constructive criticism into training routines for continuous growth
    *   Using visual feedback to reinforce proper body positioning, balance, and ball striking technique

8. Transferring Technique to Game Situations:
    *   Applying perfected shooting technique in match scenarios
    *   Managing the pressure and speed of decision-making during games
    *   Replicating training exercises and drills in game situations to enhance performance
    *   Building confidence and trust in shooting technique through successful game experiences

Perfecting the shooting technique is essential for goal-scoring proficiency in soccer. By focusing on body positioning, balance, and striking the ball cleanly, players can elevate the accuracy, power, and consistency of their shots. Through dedicated practice, repetition, and the integration of feedback and video analysis, players can refine their shooting technique and effectively transfer it to match situations. Mastering these elements not only enhances a player's ability to score goals but also contributes to their overall effectiveness and impact on the field.

The role of footwork in generating power and accuracy

Footwork is a critical aspect of shooting in soccer, directly impacting the power and accuracy of a shot. This chapter focuses on understanding the role of footwork in maximizing shooting effectiveness. By mastering footwork techniques, players can generate greater power, improve shot accuracy, and become more lethal goal-scorers.

1. Generating Power through Proper Footwork:
   - Understanding how footwork contributes to power in shooting
   - Techniques for generating momentum and transferring weight into the shot
   - Utilizing a strong plant foot and pushing off for explosive power
   - Coordinating footwork with the striking motion to maximize shot velocity

2. Establishing a Balanced Base:
   - The importance of balance in footwork for power and accuracy
   - Techniques for achieving a stable and balanced stance before shooting
   - Positioning the body to ensure weight distribution and stability
   - Utilizing the non-kicking foot for balance and support during the shot

3. Incorporating Quick and Agile Footwork:
   - The role of quick and agile footwork in creating shooting opportunities
   - Techniques for rapid directional changes and explosive acceleration
   - Developing agility through ladder drills, cone exercises, and quick footwork drills
   - Applying quick footwork to create space and evade defenders for a clear shot

4. Timing and Coordination with the Ball:
   - Understanding the importance of timing footwork with ball contact
   - Coordinating footwork and striking the ball at the optimal moment
   - Techniques for adjusting footwork based on the pace and trajectory of the ball
   - Practicing timing and coordination through drills and game simulations

5. Adjusting Footwork for Different Types of Shots:
   - Adapting footwork based on the type of shot being executed
   - Techniques for adjusting footwork for volleys, half-volleys, and one-touch shots
   - Modifying footwork for shots taken from different angles and positions
   - Analyzing and replicating footwork patterns of successful goal-scorers

6. Developing Explosiveness and Speed:
   - Enhancing explosive power through specific footwork drills and exercises
   - Incorporating plyometric exercises to improve foot speed and agility
   - Utilizing resistance training to develop leg strength and power in footwork
   - Integrating speed and agility drills to improve overall quickness on the field

7. Maintaining Balance and Stability under Pressure:
   - Techniques for maintaining balance and stability in dynamic game situations
   - Adapting footwork to maintain control and accuracy while under defensive pressure
   - Developing the ability to adjust footwork on uneven or challenging playing surfaces
   - Practicing shooting under pressure to simulate game scenarios and improve footwork efficiency

8. Game Simulation and Decision-Making:
   - Integrating footwork into game simulations and match-specific drills
   - Improving decision-making by considering footwork options based on the situation
   - Enhancing footwork efficiency by training with realistic game scenarios
   - Transferring mastered footwork techniques into match situations for increased effectiveness

Footwork is a crucial element in generating power and accuracy in shooting. By understanding its role and mastering the techniques discussed in this chapter, players can enhance their shooting abilities and become more lethal goal-scorers. Developing explosive power, maintaining balance and stability, adapting footwork to different types of shots, and refining decision-making under pressure all contribute to footwork efficiency. Through dedicated practice, drills, and game simulations, players can elevate their footwork skills and utilize them effectively to maximize power and accuracy, leading to greater success in goal-scoring.

Different shooting techniques: laces, instep, volleys, and chips

Mastering a variety of shooting techniques is essential for becoming a versatile and effective goal-scorer in soccer. This chapter explores different shooting techniques, including laces, instep, volleys, and chips. By understanding and practicing these techniques, players can expand their goal-scoring repertoire and adapt to different game situations.

1. Laces Technique:
   - Understanding the laces technique and its applications in shooting
   - Positioning the foot and striking the ball with the laces for power and accuracy
   - Techniques for generating backspin and swerve on the ball
   - Tips for maintaining balance and body control during laces shots

2. Instep Technique:
   - Exploring the instep technique and its benefits in shooting
   - Proper foot placement and striking the ball with the instep for precision
   - Utilizing the instep technique for controlled, low-driven shots
   - Adjusting body positioning and follow-through for optimal instep shots

3. Volleys:
   - The technique and advantages of volleying the ball for goal-scoring
   - Techniques for timing and striking volleys with accuracy and power
   - Adjusting footwork and body positioning for volleys from different heights

- Practicing volleys to improve coordination and develop quick reaction times

4. Chips:
   - The art of chipping the ball for finesse and precision in goal-scoring
   - Techniques for lofting the ball over the goalkeeper and into the net
   - Adjusting body position, foot angle, and follow-through for chip shots
   - Developing touch and feel through chip shot drills and practice scenarios

5. Choosing the Right Technique for the Situation:
   - Understanding when to utilize each shooting technique based on the game situation
   - Analyzing factors such as distance, angle, and goalkeeper positioning
   - Assessing the time available for shot execution and choosing the appropriate technique
   - Practicing decision-making and adapting shooting techniques in game simulations

6. Developing Technique through Drills and Training:
   - Incorporating specific drills to improve proficiency in different shooting techniques
   - Practicing laces, instep, volley, and chip shots in controlled training environments
   - Incorporating shooting technique drills into game-like scenarios for realistic practice

- Receiving feedback and guidance from coaches and teammates to refine technique

7. Real-Life Examples and Analysis:
   - Analyzing successful goal-scoring moments from professional matches
   - Examining the shooting techniques utilized by top goal-scorers
   - Learning from the technique and execution of renowned goal-scoring specialists
   - Extracting key principles and applying them to personal shooting technique development

8. Game-Specific Application:
   - Transferring mastered shooting techniques to match situations
   - Identifying opportunities to utilize different techniques during games
   - Adjusting shooting technique based on real-time game dynamics and defensive pressure
   - Developing the ability to execute various techniques instinctively and under pressure

Mastering different shooting techniques such as laces, instep, volleys, and chips enhances a player's goal-scoring repertoire and adaptability on the field. By understanding the mechanics, practicing drills, and analyzing real-life examples, players can refine their execution and decision-making in different game situations. Through dedicated training and game-specific application, players can unleash the full potential of these techniques, increasing their effectiveness as goal-scorers and contributing to their team's success.

Developing the weak foot for shooting

Developing proficiency with the weak foot is crucial for becoming a well-rounded and unpredictable goal-scorer in soccer. This chapter focuses on strategies and exercises to enhance shooting abilities with the weaker foot. By dedicating time and effort to developing the weak foot, players can increase their goal-scoring options and maintain a competitive edge on the field.

1. Embracing the Importance of the Weak Foot:

   - Understanding the advantages of a strong weak foot in goal-scoring
   - Recognizing the impact of two-footedness on a player's versatility and unpredictability
   - Overcoming the psychological barriers associated with using the weak foot
   - Setting goals and committing to the development of the weaker foot

2. Building Weak Foot Strength and Coordination:

   - Utilizing specific exercises to improve the strength and coordination of the weak foot
   - Practicing dribbling drills with the weak foot to improve ball control

- Incorporating passing and receiving exercises to develop precision and touch
- Utilizing weaker foot-specific shooting drills to enhance shooting technique and power

3. Repetitive Practice and Muscle Memory:

   - Understanding the importance of repetition in developing the weak foot
   - Engaging in deliberate and focused practice to reinforce muscle memory
   - Incorporating weak foot shooting drills into regular training sessions
   - Gradually increasing the difficulty and intensity of weak foot exercises

4. Mental Conditioning for the Weak Foot:

   - Cultivating a positive mindset and belief in the potential of the weak foot
   - Using visualization and mental imagery to develop confidence in weak foot shooting
   - Setting specific goals and targets for weak foot performance in training and matches
   - Celebrating successes and milestones achieved with the weak foot to boost motivation

5. Transferable Skills from the Strong Foot:

   - Identifying skills and techniques from the strong foot that can be transferred to the weak foot

- Analyzing shooting mechanics and footwork patterns of the strong foot
- Practicing mirror exercises to replicate strong foot movements with the weak foot
- Incorporating strong foot training principles into weak foot development routines

6. Game Simulations and Match-Specific Training:

- Integrating weak foot training into game simulations and match-specific drills
- Emphasizing the use of the weak foot during small-sided games and practice matches
- Practicing shooting scenarios that specifically require the use of the weak foot
- Seeking opportunities in matches to utilize the weak foot and reinforce training progress

7. Seeking Feedback and Guidance:

- Utilizing feedback from coaches, trainers, and teammates to identify areas for improvement
- Seeking technical guidance on proper weak foot shooting technique
- Analyzing weak foot performance through video analysis and self-assessment
- Incorporating feedback into training routines to refine weak foot shooting mechanics

8.   Patience and Perseverance:

-   Recognizing that developing the weak foot is a gradual process that requires patience
-   Embracing setbacks and learning from mistakes as part of the development journey
-   Celebrating small victories and improvements along the way
-   Maintaining dedication and consistency in weak foot training to achieve long-term success

Developing proficiency with the weak foot is a valuable asset for any goal-scorer in soccer. By employing specific exercises, mental conditioning, and match-specific training, players can enhance their shooting abilities with the weaker foot. Embracing the challenges and committing to consistent practice will lead to significant progress over time. By focusing on the development of the weak foot, players can broaden their goal-scoring options, surprise opponents, and become more complete and versatile attackers on the field.

Chapter 3: Mastering Accuracy and Placement

The importance of accuracy in finishing

Accuracy in finishing is a critical aspect of goal-scoring in soccer. This chapter explores the significance of accuracy and precision when executing shots on goal. By emphasizing accuracy, players can increase their chances of converting scoring opportunities into goals and contribute to their team's success.

1. The Impact of Accuracy in Goal-Scoring:
   - Understanding how accuracy directly affects the success rate of finishing
   - Recognizing the importance of hitting specific target areas in the goal
   - Analyzing the correlation between accuracy and goal-scoring efficiency
   - Identifying the advantages of accurate finishing in different game situations

2. Enhancing Shot Placement:
   - Techniques for precise shot placement in various target areas of the goal
   - Utilizing the corners and sides of the goal to maximize scoring opportunities
   - Adjusting shot power and body positioning to increase accuracy
   - Practicing drills and exercises that focus on shot placement and target selection

3. Developing Consistent Ball Contact:
   - The significance of consistent ball contact for accurate finishing
   - Techniques for striking the ball cleanly and consistently
   - Maintaining a consistent follow-through to improve shot accuracy
   - Incorporating drills that emphasize ball contact and develop muscle memory

4. Timing and Anticipation:
   - The role of timing and anticipation in achieving accuracy in finishing
   - Reading the game to anticipate goal-scoring opportunities
   - Adjusting body positioning and footwork to align with the ball's trajectory
   - Developing a sense of timing through game simulations and match-specific training

5. Controlling Shot Power for Accuracy:
   - Understanding the relationship between shot power and accuracy
   - Techniques for striking the right balance between power and control
   - Adjusting shooting technique to decrease shot power for more precise finishing
   - Practicing controlled shooting exercises to improve accuracy at different power levels

6. Incorporating Decision-Making for Accuracy:
   - Analyzing decision-making processes in relation to accurate finishing
   - Assessing the best shooting option based on defender positioning and goalkeeper movement
   - Developing the ability to make quick and accurate decisions under pressure
   - Utilizing peripheral vision and spatial awareness to identify open goal areas

7. Practicing Under Pressure:
   - Simulating game-like pressure in training drills and exercises
   - Incorporating time constraints and defensive pressure during shooting practice
   - Developing composure and accuracy in high-pressure scenarios
   - Training with teammates to replicate game situations and improve accuracy in finishing

8. Analyzing and Learning from Mistakes:
   - Recognizing the value of analyzing missed opportunities and inaccurate finishes
   - Identifying common mistakes and areas for improvement in finishing accuracy
   - Learning from past errors to adjust technique and decision-making for better accuracy
   - Utilizing video analysis and feedback to refine finishing technique

The importance of accuracy in finishing cannot be overstated in soccer. By focusing on shot placement, consistent ball contact, timing, and decision-making, players can enhance their accuracy in front of goal. Accuracy increases the likelihood of converting scoring opportunities and ultimately contributes to a player's goal-scoring efficiency. Through deliberate practice, game simulations, and the analysis of mistakes, players can improve their accuracy in finishing and become more lethal goal-scorers, greatly benefiting their team's overall success.

Techniques for placing shots in different areas of the goal

Placing shots accurately in different areas of the goal is crucial for goal-scoring success in soccer. This section explores various techniques that players can employ to achieve precision and maximize their scoring opportunities. By mastering these techniques, players can become more versatile and effective in finishing.

1. Near Post Placement:
   - Recognizing the advantage of near post shots in surprising goalkeepers
   - Adjusting body positioning and footwork to aim towards the near post
   - Striking the ball with the appropriate power and precision to beat the goalkeeper at the near post
   - Practicing angled shots towards the near post to develop accuracy and confidence in this placement

2. Far Post Placement:
   - Identifying situations where far post shots can catch goalkeepers off guard
   - Adjusting body position and footwork to direct the ball towards the far post
   - Striking the ball with the correct amount of power and curve to reach the far post
   - Practicing shots that curl or bend towards the far post to develop accuracy in this placement

3. Low Driven Shots:
   - Recognizing the effectiveness of low-driven shots in evading goalkeepers
   - Adjusting body position and footwork to strike the ball with the instep or laces
   - Maintaining a low follow-through to keep the shot close to the ground
   - Practicing drills that emphasize accuracy and power in low-driven shots

4. High Placed Shots:
   - Identifying situations where high-placed shots can exploit space or goalkeeper positioning
   - Adjusting body position and footwork to generate height and lift in the shot
   - Striking the ball with the appropriate power and trajectory to reach the desired height
   - Practicing shots that rise and dip to develop accuracy in high-placed shots

5. Corner Placement:
   - Recognizing the advantage of placing shots in the corners of the goal
   - Adjusting body position and footwork to target the corners
   - Striking the ball with precision and power to reach the desired corner
   - Practicing shots that target different corners of the goal to develop accuracy in corner placement

6. Top Bins Placement:
   - Identifying situations where aiming for the top corners of the goal can be advantageous
   - Adjusting body position and footwork to generate height and accuracy in the shot
   - Striking the ball with power and precision to beat the goalkeeper in the top corners
   - Practicing shots that rise and find the top bins to develop accuracy in this placement

7. Back Post Placement:
   - Recognizing the opportunities to place shots towards the back post area
   - Adjusting body position and footwork to direct the ball towards the back post
   - Striking the ball with the appropriate power and accuracy to reach the back post
   - Practicing shots that curl or bend towards the back post to develop accuracy in this placement

8. Combination Placements:
   - Understanding the effectiveness of combining different shot placements in specific situations
   - Recognizing when to mix near post, far post, high, or low shots for optimal results
   - Adapting body position, footwork, and striking technique to execute combination placements
   - Practicing drills that involve combining different shot placements to develop versatility and decision-making skills

The ability to place shots accurately in different areas of the goal is a vital skill for goal-scoring proficiency in soccer. By mastering techniques for near post, far post, low-driven, high, corner, top bins, back post, and combination placements, players can become more versatile and unpredictable finishers. Through dedicated practice, repetition, and game-specific simulations, players can develop the necessary accuracy and precision to maximize their goal-scoring opportunities. By understanding and implementing these techniques, players can elevate their finishing abilities and significantly contribute to their team's success.

Shooting drills and exercises to improve accuracy

1. Target Practice:
   - Set up targets in different areas of the goal, such as the corners or top bins.

- Take shots from various distances and angles, aiming to hit the targets consistently.
- Start with larger targets and gradually decrease their size to increase difficulty and precision.
- Repeat the drill from different positions on the field to simulate game scenarios.

2. Shooting Gates:
   - Set up two cones or poles to create a narrow gate in front of the goal.
   - Practice shooting through the gate from different angles and distances.
   - Focus on accuracy, trying to hit the target between the gates consistently.
   - Increase the challenge by decreasing the width of the gate or adding a time limit to complete the drill.

3. One-Touch Finishing:
   - Set up a passing sequence with a teammate or coach.
   - Receive a pass and aim to shoot with accuracy using only one touch.
   - Emphasize quick decision-making and accurate finishing.
   - Vary the distance, angle, and speed of the passes to challenge your ability to react and place shots accurately.

4. Rapid Fire:
   - Set up multiple balls in front of the goal or have a teammate or coach feed you balls quickly.

- Take shots in rapid succession, focusing on accuracy and quick decision-making.
- Aim to hit different target areas of the goal with each shot.
- Gradually increase the speed and intensity of the drill to simulate game-like situations.

5. Controlled Power Shots:
   - Stand at a moderate distance from the goal and focus on controlled power shots.
   - Aim for accuracy by striking the ball with the appropriate power and technique.
   - Practice different shooting techniques, such as laces, instep, or volleys, to develop accuracy with each technique.
   - Challenge yourself by placing targets in specific areas of the goal and attempting to hit them consistently.

6. Penalty Kick Practice:
   - Simulate penalty kick situations by setting up a goal and a goalkeeper.
   - Focus on accuracy by aiming for specific areas of the goal.
   - Experiment with different shooting techniques and placements to develop versatility.
   - Practice under pressure by setting goals or consequences for successful or missed shots.

7. Shooting with Obstacles:
   - Set up cones or obstacles in front of the goal, creating challenging shooting scenarios.

- Practice shooting around or over the obstacles, aiming for accuracy.
- Incorporate dribbling or quick footwork before taking the shot to simulate real-game situations.
- Vary the positioning and arrangement of the obstacles to develop adaptability and accuracy.

8. Match-Specific Finishing:
   - Participate in small-sided games or practice matches with an emphasis on finishing.
   - Apply shooting techniques and accuracy under game-like conditions.
   - React quickly to scoring opportunities and make precise decisions on shot placement.
   - Analyze and reflect on missed opportunities to identify areas for improvement.

Improving shooting accuracy requires consistent practice and dedication. By incorporating these shooting drills and exercises into training sessions, players can develop their accuracy and become more proficient goal-scorers. Remember to focus on technique, target placement, and varying difficulty levels to continually challenge yourself. Regular repetition and game-specific simulations will help translate improved accuracy into match situations, contributing to your overall goal-scoring success.

Tips for shooting under pressure

Shooting under pressure is a crucial skill for goal-scorers to possess. The ability to maintain composure and execute accurate shots in high-pressure situations can greatly contribute to a player's success. Here are some tips to help you improve your shooting under pressure:

1. Mental Preparation:

   - Visualize success: Before taking the shot, visualize yourself scoring and executing the shot with precision. Imagine yourself remaining calm and focused under pressure.

   - Develop a routine: Establish a pre-shot routine that helps you relax, clear your mind, and build confidence. Consistently following this routine can help you stay composed in pressure situations.

2. Stay Calm and Focused:

   - Control your breathing: Take deep breaths to calm your nerves and maintain focus. Slow, controlled breathing helps regulate heart rate and keeps you composed.

   - Block out distractions: Concentrate solely on the task at hand. Avoid letting external factors or the presence of opponents affect your focus and decision-making.

3. Practice Under Pressure:

- Simulate game scenarios: Incorporate pressure situations into your training sessions. Practice shooting drills and small-sided games where you have limited time and space to shoot.

- Replicate match conditions: Train with loud noises, crowd noises, or teammates applying defensive pressure to simulate the pressure of a game environment. Familiarize yourself with performing under similar conditions.

4. Quick Decision-Making:

- Anticipate opportunities: Stay aware of the game flow and anticipate scoring chances. Position yourself well in advance to be ready for the decisive moment.

- Be decisive: Trust your instincts and make quick decisions. Overthinking can hinder your ability to execute accurate shots under pressure.

5. Improve Technique and Muscle Memory:

- Consistent practice: Regularly practice shooting drills and exercises to refine your technique. The more you repeat the motions, the more comfortable and automatic they become.

- Muscle memory: Develop muscle memory by repeating proper shooting techniques in various situations. This allows you to execute shots with accuracy even when under pressure.

6. Develop Confidence:

    •   Positive self-talk: Encourage yourself with positive self-talk and affirmations. Replace negative thoughts with confident and empowering statements.

    •   Draw from past successes: Reflect on previous successful goal-scoring moments to boost your confidence. Remind yourself of your capabilities and the times you've performed under pressure.

7. Adaptability and Versatility:

    •   Vary your shot placements: Practice shooting in different target areas of the goal to develop versatility. This allows you to adapt your shooting technique based on the goalkeeper's position or defensive pressure.

    •   Develop multiple shooting techniques: Master various shooting techniques, such as laces, instep, volleys, and chips, to have a wider range of options when shooting under pressure.

8. Learn from Mistakes:

    •   Embrace setbacks as learning opportunities: If you miss a chance under pressure, use it as a learning experience. Analyze what went wrong and focus on improving rather than dwelling on the mistake.

    •   Adjust and adapt: Use feedback from coaches or teammates to refine your technique and decision-making in pressure situations. Continuously work on areas that need improvement.

Shooting under pressure takes practice, experience, and mental strength. By implementing these tips and regularly exposing yourself to pressure situations in training, you can enhance your ability to execute accurate shots when it matters most.

Chapter 4: Power and Long-Range Shooting

Generating power through proper technique and body mechanics

Generating power in your shots is essential for a potent and effective goal-scoring ability. It requires mastering proper technique and utilizing efficient body mechanics. Here are some tips to help you generate power through correct technique and body mechanics:

1. Body Positioning:
    *   Square your shoulders to the target: Align your body and shoulders directly towards the goal. This allows for optimal transfer of power from your body to the shot.
    *   Position your non-kicking foot: Place your non-kicking foot next to the ball, slightly behind it, for stability and balance. This foot serves as the anchor for generating power.

2. Backswing and Loading:
    *   Take a controlled backswing: Bring your kicking leg back while maintaining balance and control. Avoid overexaggerated or excessive backswings, as they can hinder accuracy and timing.
    *   Load your striking leg: As you bring your leg back, flex your kicking knee and load it with energy. This creates potential energy to be released in the forward motion of the shot.

3. Hip Rotation and Torque:
   - Engage your core and hips: Initiate the forward motion by rotating your hips and engaging your core muscles. This generates rotational force and adds power to the shot.
   - Create torque with your upper body: As you swing your leg forward, twist your upper body in the opposite direction to create torque. This additional rotational force adds power to your shot.

4. Striking Technique:
   - Make clean contact with the ball: Aim to strike the ball with the center or top portion of your foot. This provides a larger surface area for contact and allows for better control and power.
   - Follow through with your kicking leg: After striking the ball, continue the forward motion with your kicking leg. This ensures a complete and powerful follow-through, maximizing shot power.

5. Timing and Weight Transfer:
   - Time your shot properly: Coordinate your body movements and the striking of the ball for optimal timing. Practice your timing to strike the ball at the right moment for maximum power.
   - Transfer your weight forward: As you swing your leg forward, shift your weight from the back foot to the front foot. This transfers your body's momentum into the shot, adding power.

6. Leg and Ankle Strength:
   - Strengthen your leg muscles: Incorporate exercises such as squats, lunges, and plyometrics to develop leg strength. Stronger leg muscles allow for more explosive shots.
   - Develop ankle stability: Strengthen your ankle muscles and improve stability through exercises like ankle rotations and balancing drills. A stable ankle allows for better control and power in your shots.

7. Explosive Movement Training:
   - Include explosive movements in your training regimen: Incorporate exercises like box jumps, medicine ball throws, and sprinting to develop explosive power in your legs.
   - Combine strength training with speed and agility drills: Work on combining strength training exercises with speed and agility drills to improve your overall power and quickness on the field.

8. Practice and Repetition:
   - Consistently practice shooting technique: Regularly dedicate time to practice your shooting technique, focusing on generating power. Repetition helps develop muscle memory and improves your ability to generate power efficiently.
   - Apply proper technique in game-like scenarios: Incorporate shooting drills and match simulations into your training sessions to replicate game situations. This allows you to practice generating power under

varying levels of pressure and from different positions on the field.

Remember, generating power through proper technique and body mechanics takes time and practice. Focus on mastering these fundamentals and gradually increase your power by incorporating strength and explosive training into your regimen. With dedication and consistent effort, you can significantly enhance the power and effectiveness of your shots, becoming a more potent goal-scorer on the field.

Exercises to develop leg strength and explosive shooting

Developing leg strength and explosive shooting requires a combination of strength training and explosive exercises that target the lower body muscles. Here are some exercises that can help you improve leg strength and develop a more explosive shooting ability:

1. Squats:
   - Stand with your feet shoulder-width apart.
   - Lower your body by bending your knees and pushing your hips back as if sitting down.
   - Keep your chest up and back straight.
   - Return to the starting position by pushing through your heels and extending your knees and hips.
   - Perform squats with or without weights, gradually increasing the load as your strength improves.

2. Lunges:
   - Stand with your feet hip-width apart.
   - Step forward with one leg and lower your body until both knees are bent at a 90-degree angle.
   - Push through your front heel to return to the starting position.
   - Repeat on the other leg.
   - To add intensity, hold dumbbells or use a barbell across your shoulders.

3. Deadlifts:
   - Stand with your feet hip-width apart, holding a barbell or dumbbells in front of your thighs.
   - Hinge at your hips and lower the weights towards the ground while maintaining a flat back.
   - Keep your knees slightly bent and your chest lifted.
   - Push through your heels and engage your glutes and hamstrings to lift the weights back up.
   - Be mindful of maintaining proper form and start with lighter weights before progressing to heavier loads.

4. Plyometric Exercises:
   - Box Jumps: Stand in front of a sturdy box or platform. Jump onto the box, landing with both feet simultaneously. Step back down and repeat.
   - Split Squat Jumps: Assume a lunge position with one foot forward and the other foot behind you. Explosively jump up, switching the position of your feet mid-air, and land in a lunge with the opposite leg forward.

- Broad Jumps: Stand with your feet shoulder-width apart. Bend your knees and swing your arms back. Explosively jump forward, extending your hips and swinging your arms forward for momentum. Land softly and repeat.

5. Single-Leg Exercises:
   - Single-Leg Squats: Stand on one leg with the other leg extended in front of you. Lower your body by bending the knee of the standing leg, keeping your chest up and back straight. Push through the heel to return to the starting position. Repeat on the other leg.
   - Bulgarian Split Squats: Stand facing away from a bench or elevated platform with one foot resting on it behind you. Lower your body by bending the front knee until the back knee almost touches the ground. Push through the front heel to return to the starting position. Repeat on the other leg.

6. Resistance Band Exercises:
   - Resistance Band Squats: Place a resistance band just above your knees. Perform squats while maintaining tension on the band. This helps strengthen the hip muscles, which are essential for explosive shooting.
   - Lateral Band Walks: Step into a resistance band and place it just above your knees. Take small steps sideways, maintaining tension on the band throughout. This exercise targets the hip abductors, which are important for stability and power in shooting.

7. Kettlebell Swings:
   - Stand with your feet shoulder-width apart, holding a kettlebell with both hands between your legs.
   - Hinge at your hips and swing the kettlebell up to chest level, maintaining a strong and stable core.
   - Squeeze your glutes at the top of the movement, then let the kettlebell swing back down between your legs.
   - Control the movement and repeat for the desired number of reps.

8. Explosive Shooting Drills:
   - Practice shooting while incorporating explosive movements, such as jumping or sprinting, before taking the shot. This helps simulate game situations where explosive power is required.
   - Perform shooting drills with time constraints or under defensive pressure to replicate the pressure of game scenarios and improve your ability to shoot explosively.

Remember to warm up properly before engaging in these exercises and focus on maintaining proper form throughout. Start with lighter weights or lower-intensity variations and gradually progress to more challenging variations as your strength and technique improve. Consistency and dedication to these exercises will help you develop leg strength and explosive shooting, ultimately enhancing your goal-scoring ability on the field.

Techniques for shooting from distance and outside the box

Shooting from distance and outside the box can be a potent weapon for goal-scoring, allowing you to surprise goalkeepers and increase your scoring opportunities. Here are some techniques to help you improve your shooting from distance:

1. Proper Body Positioning:
   - Approach the ball with your body slightly over it, leaning forward.
   - Align your body and shoulders towards the target.
   - Plant your non-kicking foot next to the ball and slightly behind it to provide stability.

2. Striking the Ball:
   - Use the laces or instep of your foot to strike the ball.
   - Aim to strike the lower half of the ball to generate lift and trajectory.
   - Focus on hitting the ball cleanly and with power to maximize distance and speed.

3. Timing and Follow-Through:
   - Time your shot to strike the ball at the optimal moment as it comes into your range.
   - Maintain a controlled and fluid follow-through, extending your kicking leg fully towards the target.
   - Keep your head down and your eyes on the ball throughout the shot.

4. Generating Power:
   - Transfer your weight forward as you strike the ball, using your entire body to generate power.
   - Rotate your hips and engage your core muscles to add force to the shot.
   - Focus on a quick and explosive leg swing to generate power while maintaining accuracy.

5. Backspin and Trajectory:
   - Use the correct technique to create backspin on the ball for improved control and accuracy.
   - Aim to strike the ball with a slightly downward angle to generate a trajectory that dips and makes it difficult for the goalkeeper to save.

6. Visualization and Decision-Making:
   - Anticipate shooting opportunities from distance and outside the box.
   - Assess the positioning of the goalkeeper, defenders, and available space before taking the shot.
   - Visualize the desired placement and trajectory of the shot before executing it.

7. Practice Shooting from Distance:
   - Set up shooting drills specifically designed to improve shooting from distance.
   - Practice striking the ball with power and accuracy from various distances and angles outside the box.
   - Incorporate game-like scenarios, such as shooting under defensive pressure or with limited time, to simulate real match situations.

8. Game Awareness and Shot Selection:
   - Develop a sense of game awareness to identify optimal situations for shooting from distance.
   - Recognize when shooting from distance is a better option than trying to dribble or pass.
   - Make quick decisions on whether to shoot or adjust your position to create a better shooting opportunity.

9. Analyze and Learn from Feedback:
   - Seek feedback from coaches, teammates, or video analysis to identify areas for improvement.
   - Analyze your shooting technique and shot placement to refine your technique.
   - Learn from missed shots and adjust your technique and decision-making accordingly.

Shooting from distance requires practice, confidence, and the ability to strike the ball with power and accuracy. With consistent training, specific drills, and game awareness, you can develop the skills necessary to become a threat from distance and outside the box, adding another dimension to your goal-scoring ability.

Shooting with power while maintaining accuracy

Shooting with power while maintaining accuracy is a crucial skill for goal-scorers in soccer. Balancing both aspects allows you to generate enough force to beat the goalkeeper while still placing your shots precisely. Here are some techniques to help you achieve powerful and accurate shooting:

1. Proper Technique:

    -   Focus on a solid foundation: Plant your non-kicking foot next to the ball and slightly behind it for stability and balance.

    -   Approach the ball with your body slightly over it, leaning forward.

    -   Keep your head down and eyes on the ball throughout the shot.

2. Generate Leg Power:

    -   Engage your leg muscles: Utilize the power in your leg muscles, particularly your quadriceps and hip flexors, to generate explosive force.

    -   Load your kicking leg: As you bring your leg back, flex your kicking knee and load it with energy. This potential energy will be released in the forward motion of the shot.

3. Timing and Follow-Through:

    -   Time your shot correctly: Coordinate your body movements and the striking of the ball for optimal timing. Practice your timing to strike the ball at the right moment to maximize power.

    -   Maintain a controlled follow-through: Extend your kicking leg fully toward the target, emphasizing a complete follow-through while maintaining balance and control.

4. Striking Technique:

    - Use the laces or instep of your foot: Striking the ball with the laces or instep provides the surface area and stability required for powerful shots.

    - Aim to hit the ball's center or slightly below its equator: This helps generate lift and prevents the ball from rising too high.

    - Maintain a clean contact with the ball: Strive for a clean strike, hitting the ball cleanly and squarely for optimal power and accuracy.

5. Weight Transfer and Core Engagement:

    - Shift your weight forward: As you swing your leg forward to strike the ball, transfer your weight from your back foot to your front foot. This transfers your body's momentum into the shot, adding power.

    - Engage your core: Initiate the forward motion by rotating your hips and engaging your core muscles. This rotational force contributes to the power behind your shot.

6. Shot Placement:

    - Visualize your target: Before shooting, mentally visualize the desired target area.

- Pick your spots: Instead of aiming for sheer power, identify specific target areas in the goal where accuracy is essential. Focus on precision and shot placement, combining power with accuracy.

7. Practice Shooting Drills:

- Incorporate shooting drills that emphasize power and accuracy: Set up shooting drills with targets or specific zones in the goal to practice hitting those areas with maximum power while maintaining accuracy.

- Vary distances and angles: Practice shooting from different distances and angles to develop the ability to generate power accurately from various positions on the field.

8. Game-Like Scenarios:

- Simulate game situations in training: Replicate scenarios where shooting with power and accuracy is required, such as shooting under defensive pressure or with limited time and space.

- Implement shooting exercises during small-sided games or match simulations: This helps develop the ability to make quick decisions and execute powerful, accurate shots under game-like conditions.

9. Analyze and Learn from Feedback:

- Seek feedback from coaches, teammates, or video analysis to identify areas for improvement.

- Analyze your shooting technique and shot placement to refine your accuracy and power.

- Learn from missed shots and adjust your technique and decision-making accordingly.

The key is to find the balance between power and accuracy. Consistent practice, focused training, and a combination of proper technique, timing, and core engagement will help you develop the ability to shoot with both power and accuracy, ultimately enhancing your goal-scoring prowess on the field.

Chapter 5: Finishing in Various Game Situations

Techniques for finishing one-on-one with the goalkeeper

One-on-one situations with the goalkeeper offer an excellent opportunity for goal-scoring, but they can also be challenging. Here are some techniques and tips to help you improve your finishing ability in one-on-one situations:

1. Stay Calm and Composed:
   - Keep a cool head and remain composed when faced with a one-on-one situation.
   - Avoid rushing your decision-making and shooting technique.
   - Maintain focus and confidence in your ability to finish.

2. Assess the Goalkeeper:
   - Observe the positioning of the goalkeeper: Take note of their body positioning, whether they are off their line or coming out quickly.
   - Look for any gaps or weaknesses in their positioning that you can exploit.

3. Change of Pace and Direction:
   - Use changes of pace and direction to create space: Utilize quick bursts of acceleration or changes in direction to create separation from the goalkeeper.
   - Take advantage of your agility and speed to gain an advantage in the one-on-one situation.

4. Use Body Feints and Fakes:
   - Employ body feints and fakes to deceive the goalkeeper: Use subtle body movements to make the goalkeeper commit early or shift their weight in the wrong direction.
   - Utilize shoulder drops, hip shifts, or eye movements to manipulate the goalkeeper and create openings for your shot.

5. Use Both Feet:
   - Develop proficiency with both feet: Be comfortable finishing with either foot to keep the goalkeeper guessing and increase your options in one-on-one situations.
   - Practice shooting and dribbling exercises with your weaker foot to improve its effectiveness in finishing.

6. Placement and Accuracy:
   - Aim for precision and placement: Instead of relying solely on power, focus on accurate shot placement to beat the goalkeeper.
   - Identify the areas of the goal that are more difficult for the goalkeeper to cover, such as the corners or the area just out of their reach.
   - Practice shooting to specific target areas during training to enhance your accuracy in finishing.

7. Change the Angle of Attack:
   - Alter the angle of your approach: As you approach the goalkeeper, change the angle of your attack to open up different shooting opportunities.

- Cut inside or go wide to create different angles and challenge the goalkeeper's positioning.

8. Maintain Eye Contact:
   - Keep your eyes on the goalkeeper: Maintain eye contact to observe their movement and reactions.
   - Use this information to adjust your shooting technique or direction at the last moment to catch the goalkeeper off guard.

9. Practice One-on-One Drills:
   - Set up drills specifically designed for one-on-one scenarios: Work on dribbling past a defender and finishing against a goalkeeper in controlled practice situations.
   - Practice with varying levels of defensive pressure to simulate real-game scenarios.

10. Analyze and Learn:
    - Review your performances and seek feedback: Analyze your finishing attempts in one-on-one situations to identify areas for improvement.
    - Seek feedback from coaches, teammates, or video analysis to gain insights into your decision-making and technique.
    - Learn from each experience and apply those lessons to future one-on-one situations.

Finishing one-on-one with the goalkeeper requires a combination of technical proficiency, tactical awareness, and mental composure. By practicing these techniques, developing both feet, and analyzing your performances, you can enhance your ability to convert one-on-one opportunities into goals and become a more effective goal-scorer.

Understanding different angles and positions for finishing

When it comes to finishing in soccer, understanding the different angles and positions from which you can score is crucial. By recognizing and utilizing these angles effectively, you can increase your chances of finding the back of the net. Here are some key angles and positions to consider:

1. Central Position:
   - The central position, directly in front of the goal, provides a balanced and advantageous angle for shooting.
   - It offers a wide range of target areas, allowing for more flexibility in shot placement.
   - Use this position when you have a clear path to the goal and can generate power and accuracy with your shot.

2. Near Post:
   - The near post angle refers to shooting towards the side of the goal closest to you.
   - It can be advantageous when the goalkeeper is positioned more towards the center or far post, leaving space to exploit.

- Aim for the near post with power and accuracy to catch the goalkeeper off guard and beat them from a tight angle.
3. Far Post:
   - The far post angle involves shooting towards the side of the goal furthest from you.
   - It can be effective when the goalkeeper is favoring the near post or when you want to place the ball away from their reach.
   - Striking the ball with precision and power, aiming for the far post, increases your chances of finding the back of the net.

4. High Finish:
   - The high finish angle refers to shooting towards the top portion of the goal.
   - It can be effective when the goalkeeper is positioned closer to the ground or when you want to chip the ball over them.
   - Use the correct technique to generate height and power in your shot, aiming for the upper corners of the goal.

5. Low Finish:
   - The low finish angle involves shooting towards the bottom portion of the goal.
   - It can be advantageous when the goalkeeper is taller or has difficulty getting down quickly.
   - Keep the ball close to the ground, aiming for the corners or areas where the goalkeeper has less chance of making a save.

6. Angled Shots:
   - Angled shots occur when you are shooting from positions that are not directly in front of the goal.
   - Utilize the angle to your advantage by aiming for the far or near post, depending on the goalkeeper's positioning.
   - Adjust your technique and shot power to account for the angle and maximize your chances of scoring.

7. Rebound Opportunities:
   - Rebound opportunities occur when a shot initially hits the goalpost or is saved by the goalkeeper.
   - Position yourself well to anticipate and react quickly to potential rebounds.
   - Shoot from close range with accuracy and power to capitalize on these second-chance opportunities.

8. Counterattacks and Breakaways:
   - Counterattacks and breakaways provide opportunities to finish in one-on-one situations with the goalkeeper.
   - Utilize your speed, agility, and decision-making to find the optimal angle and position to shoot from.
   - Assess the goalkeeper's position and adjust your angle of attack to create the best scoring opportunity.

Understanding and recognizing the different angles and positions for finishing requires experience, game awareness, and the ability to make quick decisions. By practicing shooting from various angles and positions in training and analyzing successful finishes, you can develop the instincts and skills necessary to be a more lethal goal-scorer.

Shooting under pressure from tight spaces and crowded defenses

Shooting under pressure from tight spaces and crowded defenses is a challenging but essential skill for goal-scorers. These situations often require quick thinking, precision, and the ability to create shooting opportunities. Here are some techniques to help you shoot effectively in tight spaces and crowded defenses:

1. Quick Decision-Making:
    *   Assess the situation: Evaluate the positioning of defenders and the goalkeeper to identify gaps or spaces to exploit.
    *   Make quick decisions: React rapidly to create shooting opportunities before defenders close down the space.

2. Body Feints and Quick Turns:
    *   Utilize body feints and quick turns to create separation: Use sudden shifts or fake movements to deceive defenders and create space for a shot.
    *   Employ shoulder drops, hip shifts, or quick direction changes to create a momentary advantage.

3. Ball Control and Close Ball Mastery:
   - Master close ball control: Develop the ability to keep the ball close to your feet and under control, even in tight spaces.
   - Utilize quick touches and close ball mastery to maneuver around defenders and find shooting lanes.

4. Precision and Placement:
   - Focus on accuracy and placement: Instead of relying solely on power, emphasize precise shot placement to beat the goalkeeper.
   - Identify small gaps or openings in the crowded defense and aim for those areas with accuracy and control.

5. Use Quick Releases:
   - Shoot with a quick release: Minimize the time between receiving the ball and taking the shot to catch defenders and the goalkeeper off guard.
   - Develop a quick and fluid shooting technique that allows for rapid execution.

6. One-Touch Finishing:
   - Practice one-touch finishing: Develop the ability to shoot accurately with only one touch, allowing you to capitalize on tight spaces and crowded defenses.
   - Work on receiving the ball and immediately shooting with precision and power.

7. Combination Play:
   - Engage in combination play with teammates: Use quick passes, one-twos, or give-and-gos to create shooting opportunities.
   - Utilize the movement and positioning of teammates to create openings in the crowded defense.

8. Awareness of Goalkeeper's Position:
   - Be aware of the goalkeeper's position: Recognize whether the goalkeeper is off their line or positioned in a specific way.
   - Adjust your shooting technique and placement to exploit any vulnerabilities or spaces that the goalkeeper leaves exposed.

9. Practice in Small-Sided Games:
   - Engage in small-sided games with limited space: Develop the ability to shoot under pressure by playing in small-sided games where tight spaces and crowded defenses are common.
   - Practice shooting with speed and accuracy in these game-like situations to enhance your skills in tight spaces.

10. Analyze and Learn:
    - Review your performances and seek feedback: Analyze your decision-making, technique, and shot placement in tight spaces and crowded defenses.
    - Seek feedback from coaches, teammates, or video analysis to gain insights into areas for improvement.

- Learn from each experience and apply those lessons to future situations.

Shooting under pressure in tight spaces and crowded defenses requires a combination of technical proficiency, quick decision-making, and precision. With practice, game awareness, and the ability to adapt to different situations, you can become more effective in finding scoring opportunities and making the most of them.

Capitalizing on rebounds and loose balls

Capitalizing on rebounds and loose balls is a valuable skill for goal-scorers in soccer. These situations often occur in the chaotic moments following a shot or a save, and being able to react quickly and efficiently can lead to goal-scoring opportunities. Here are some techniques to help you capitalize on rebounds and loose balls:

1. Anticipation and Readiness:

   - Anticipate rebounds: Position yourself in a strategic location inside the penalty area, near the goal, where rebounds are likely to occur.

   - Stay alert and ready to react: Keep your eyes on the ball and be prepared to pounce on any loose balls that come your way.

2. Quick Reaction Time:

- React swiftly to rebounds: As soon as a shot is taken or a save is made, be quick to adjust your position and make a move towards the loose ball.

- Be proactive and beat defenders to the ball by reacting faster and showing greater determination.

3. Instinctive Movements:

- Use instinctive movements: Rely on your natural reflexes and instincts to get to the loose ball before others.

- Be willing to dive, stretch, or lunge for the ball to gain an advantage over defenders and increase your chances of scoring.

4. Timing and Decision-Making:

- Time your movements: Judge the trajectory of the rebound and time your run to meet the ball at its optimal point.

- Make quick decisions: Assess the situation and decide whether to shoot, dribble, or pass based on the positioning of defenders, the goalkeeper, and your teammates.

5. Composure and Accuracy:

- Maintain composure in tight spaces: Keep calm under pressure and remain composed when finishing from close range.

- Aim for accuracy: Instead of relying solely on power, focus on placing your shot accurately, taking advantage of any gaps or weaknesses in the defense or the goalkeeper's positioning.

6. Improvisation and Creativity:

   - Be creative with your finishing: Use various techniques such as volleys, flicks, or deft touches to outwit the defense and find the back of the net.

   - Be willing to try unexpected and unconventional methods to capitalize on loose balls.

7. Practicing Rebound Scenarios:

   - Set up rebound-specific drills: Create practice scenarios where shots are taken and rebounds occur.

   - Work on reacting quickly and finishing from different angles and distances to simulate game-like situations.

8. Persistence and Determination:

   - Stay persistent: Keep hunting for loose balls and rebounds even if the initial attempt was unsuccessful.

   - Display determination and a never-give-up attitude to maximize your chances of capitalizing on second-chance opportunities.

9. Analyze and Learn:

   - Review your performances and seek feedback: Analyze your decision-making, technique, and positioning in rebound situations.

- Seek feedback from coaches, teammates, or video analysis to gain insights into areas for improvement.

- Learn from each experience and apply those lessons to future situations.

Capitalizing on rebounds and loose balls requires a combination of anticipation, quick reactions, composure, and accuracy. With practice, game awareness, and the ability to seize opportunities in chaotic moments, you can increase your goal-scoring effectiveness and become a more opportunistic striker.

Chapter 6: Goal-Scoring Movement and Positioning

Creating space and making intelligent runs to get into goal-scoring positions

Creating space and making intelligent runs to get into goal-scoring positions is a crucial skill for strikers and attacking players in soccer. By understanding how to create space and time your runs effectively, you can increase your chances of receiving the ball in dangerous areas. Here are some techniques to help you create space and make intelligent runs:

1. Off-the-Ball Movement:
   - Constantly be on the move: Avoid standing still and make continuous runs to create space for yourself and your teammates.
   - Vary your movement: Combine different types of runs, such as diagonal, curved, or straight runs, to confuse defenders and find gaps in the defense.

2. Timing and Communication:
   - Time your runs: Anticipate when your teammate is about to pass the ball and make your run accordingly. Aim to arrive at the right place at the right time.
   - Communicate with your teammates: Use verbal and non-verbal cues to signal when and where you want the ball played. Develop an understanding with your teammates to facilitate accurate passes.

3. Use Changes of Pace and Direction:
   - Employ changes of pace and direction: Mix up your speed and direction to unsettle defenders and create separation.
   - Use sudden bursts of speed to exploit gaps or to make late runs into the box when defenders are focused elsewhere.

4. Utilize Off-the-Ball Screens and Runs:
   - Take advantage of off-the-ball screens: Use your teammates' movements to create space for yourself. Make runs off their screens to confuse defenders and find open areas.
   - Make overlapping or underlapping runs: Coordinate with your teammates to make overlapping or underlapping runs, creating confusion and opportunities for through balls or cutbacks.

5. Use Lateral Movement and Drift:
   - Drift into open spaces: Move laterally across the field to find gaps between defenders or exploit space on the opposite side of the field.
   - Drift towards the back post: Time your run to drift towards the back post, where you can capitalize on crosses and cutbacks.

6. Exploit the Blindside of Defenders:
   - Make blindside runs: Time your runs to exploit the blindside of defenders, positioning yourself where they can't see you, allowing you to receive the ball unmarked.

- Aim to make runs behind the defensive line or between defenders, making it difficult for them to track your movement.

7. Create Separation and Change Directions:
   - Create separation from defenders: Use quick changes of direction, feints, or body feints to create space between yourself and the defenders.
   - Create diagonal runs: Angle your runs diagonally to create space behind the defenders and open up passing lanes.

8. Study the Opposition's Defensive Structure:
   - Analyze the opposition's defensive structure: Identify weak points, areas where defenders are less organized, or gaps that you can exploit.
   - Adjust your positioning and runs based on their defensive patterns and tendencies.

9. Practice and Game Awareness:
   - Practice off-the-ball movements: Incorporate drills that focus on off-the-ball movements and timing runs into your training sessions.
   - Develop game awareness: Pay attention to the positioning of defenders, the movement of your teammates, and the flow of the game. This awareness will help you make better decisions regarding your runs.

10. Analyze and Learn:
    - Review your performances and seek feedback: Analyze your movement, decision-making, and positioning during games or training sessions.
    - Seek feedback from coaches, teammates, or video analysis to gain insights into areas for improvement.
    - Learn from successful runs and adjustments made in previous matches to continually refine your ability to create space.

Creating space and making intelligent runs is a combination of understanding the game, good communication with teammates, and having a sense of timing. By practicing these techniques and developing your game intelligence, you can become a more effective goal-scoring threat by consistently finding yourself in dangerous positions to receive the ball and score.

Timing runs to stay onside and exploit defensive vulnerabilities

Timing runs to stay onside and exploit defensive vulnerabilities is a crucial skill for strikers and attacking players in soccer. By mastering the art of timing your runs, you can maximize your goal-scoring opportunities and take advantage of defensive weaknesses. Here are some techniques to help you time your runs effectively:

1. Monitor the Defensive Line:
   - Keep an eye on the defensive line: Pay attention to the positioning and movement of the opposing defenders.
   - Observe their line of defense and look for gaps or moments when the defensive line is not properly organized or stepping up.

2. Coordinate with Teammates:
   - Develop an understanding with your teammates: Build a connection with your midfielders or teammates who can provide through balls or long passes.
   - Communicate your intention to make runs behind the defense and coordinate your timing with their passes.

3. Use Peripheral Vision:
   - Utilize peripheral vision: Keep an eye on the ball and the positioning of your teammates, as well as the defenders and the defensive line.
   - This will allow you to assess the situation and time your run to stay onside and exploit any openings.

4. Take Advantage of Slow or Ball-Watching Defenders:
   - Exploit slow or ball-watching defenders: Identify defenders who are slower in reacting or those who get caught ball-watching.
   - Time your run to exploit the space left behind by these defenders, making it difficult for them to recover.

5. Delay Your Run:
   - Delay your run slightly: Instead of sprinting immediately, time your run to start just as the ball is played.
   - This delays your movement, making it harder for defenders to anticipate and track your run.

6. Utilize the Offside Line:
   - Familiarize yourself with the offside line: Understand the positioning of the last defender and time your run to stay level or slightly behind them.
   - Practice awareness of the offside rule and know when to time your run to beat the offside trap.

7. Employ Quick Bursts of Speed:
   - Utilize quick bursts of speed: Incorporate sudden accelerations to beat the defenders and reach the ball in time.
   - Time these bursts to coincide with the release of the pass, giving you the advantage in the race to the ball.

8. Study the Defensive Patterns:
   - Analyze the defensive patterns of the opposition: Observe how the defense moves and adjusts during different situations.
   - Identify patterns, such as defenders being pulled out of position or leaving gaps, and time your runs to exploit these vulnerabilities.

9. Practice Timing Runs in Training:
   - Incorporate timing run drills in training: Set up exercises that simulate game situations, focusing on timing your runs to stay onside and exploit defensive vulnerabilities.
   - Work with teammates to develop an understanding of each other's movements and timing.

10. Analyze and Learn:
   - Review your performances and seek feedback: Analyze your timing of runs in previous matches or training sessions.
   - Seek feedback from coaches, teammates, or video analysis to gain insights into areas for improvement.
   - Learn from successful runs and adjustments made in previous games to continually refine your ability to time your runs effectively.

Timing runs to stay onside and exploit defensive vulnerabilities requires a combination of observation, communication, and game intelligence. By practicing these techniques and continuously improving your timing, you can become a more effective and dangerous attacking player, creating scoring opportunities and capitalizing on defensive weaknesses.

Analyzing goal-scoring movements of top strikers

Analyzing the goal-scoring movements of top strikers can provide valuable insights into their techniques, positioning, and decision-making in front of goal. Here are some key aspects to consider when studying the movements of top strikers:

1. Intelligent Runs:
   - Top strikers have a keen sense of timing and anticipation, making intelligent runs to exploit spaces and create goal-scoring opportunities.
   - They make diagonal runs, curved runs, or straight runs to confuse defenders and find gaps in the defense.
   - They adjust their runs based on the movement of their teammates and the positioning of defenders to create passing options and open up space for themselves.

2. Positioning in the Box:
   - Top strikers understand the importance of positioning themselves in goal-scoring areas within the penalty box.
   - They seek positions between defenders, making it harder for them to mark or track their movements.
   - They position themselves in areas where they can receive crosses, cutbacks, or through balls with maximum efficiency.

3. Movement Off the Ball:
   - Top strikers are constantly on the move, even when they don't have the ball.

- They create separation from defenders by using quick changes of pace, feints, or body movements.
- They make runs to stretch the defense, create space for their teammates, and disrupt defensive organization.

4. Exploiting Defensive Vulnerabilities:
    - Top strikers have a knack for identifying and exploiting defensive vulnerabilities.
    - They analyze the positioning and movement of defenders to find gaps or weaknesses that can be exploited.
    - They exploit blindside runs, spaces behind the defensive line, or areas where defenders are out of position to create goal-scoring opportunities.

5. Awareness of Goalkeeper Positioning:
    - Top strikers pay close attention to the positioning and movement of the goalkeeper.
    - They identify moments when the goalkeeper is off their line or vulnerable and adjust their shooting technique and placement accordingly.
    - They aim for areas of the goal where the goalkeeper is less likely to make a save, such as the corners or the far post.

6. Instinctive Finishing:
    - Top strikers possess excellent instincts when it comes to finishing.
    - They have a natural feel for the timing, power, and placement required to score goals.

- They display composure and accuracy in front of goal, capitalizing on even the smallest scoring opportunities.

7. Movement to Create Rebound Opportunities:
   - Top strikers are proactive in their movement to create rebound opportunities.
   - They position themselves well to anticipate rebounds off the goalkeeper or the goal frame.
   - They react quickly to pounce on loose balls and capitalize on second-chance opportunities.

8. Adaptability and Versatility:
   - Top strikers can adapt their movements and style of play to different game situations and opponents.
   - They adjust their runs and positioning based on the defensive structure and tactics of the opposition.
   - They can play as lone strikers, in partnerships, or in different systems, showcasing their versatility and ability to find scoring positions in various contexts.

9. Learning from Others:
   - Studying the movements of top strikers can help you learn and incorporate their techniques into your own game.
   - Analyze their game footage, watch their positioning, runs, and decision-making in different scenarios.
   - Identify patterns, tendencies, and strategies that you can apply to improve your own goal-scoring movements.

Analyzing the goal-scoring movements of top strikers requires a keen eye for detail, patience, and the ability to break down their performances. By studying and understanding their movements, you can gain valuable insights to enhance your own goal-scoring prowess and become a more effective striker on the field.

Improving anticipation and decision-making in the final third

Improving anticipation and decision-making in the final third of the field is crucial for attacking players looking to create goal-scoring opportunities. Here are some techniques to help you enhance your anticipation and decision-making skills in the final third:

1. Study the Game:

   - Develop a deep understanding of the game: Study the tactics, patterns, and movements of both your team and the opposition.

   - Analyze the positioning of defenders, the movement of your teammates, and the spaces that open up in the final third.

   - Anticipate how the game is likely to unfold and how defenders are likely to react in different situations.

2. Improve Game Awareness:

   - Maintain awareness of your surroundings: Constantly scan the field to assess the positioning of defenders, the goalkeeper, and your teammates.

   - Keep track of available passing options, potential gaps in the defense, and goal-scoring opportunities that may arise.

3. Visualize Different Scenarios:

   - Mentally rehearse different scenarios: Imagine various situations that can occur in the final third, such as receiving a through ball, making a run into space, or creating a shooting opportunity.

   - Visualize the movements and decisions you would make in those scenarios to prepare yourself for real-time decision-making during matches.

4. Develop a Feel for Timing:

   - Enhance your timing and anticipation: Work on sensing when a pass or opportunity is about to arise.

   - Develop a feel for the game and learn to predict where the ball is going to be played or where the spaces will open up, allowing you to position yourself accordingly.

5. Analyze Defenders' Reactions:

    *   Observe defenders' reactions and tendencies: Pay attention to how defenders react to your movements and positioning.

    *   Identify patterns in their defensive behavior, such as how they shift or mark in certain situations.

    *   Exploit their weaknesses and vulnerabilities by making runs or decisions that go against their expectations.

6. Improve Decision-Making Speed:

    *   Train for quick decision-making: Practice making split-second decisions in training exercises and small-sided games.

    *   Develop the ability to analyze situations rapidly and choose the most effective option, whether it's a pass, shot, or dribble.

7. Learn from Experience:

    *   Reflect on your performances: After matches, review your decision-making in the final third.

    *   Identify areas for improvement, such as instances where you could have made better choices or anticipated the game better.

    *   Learn from both successful and unsuccessful moments, adjusting your decision-making approach accordingly.

8. Play in Small-Sided Games:

- Engage in small-sided games: Play in smaller formats of the game to increase your involvement and decision-making opportunities in the final third.

- These games provide more repetitions and allow you to experiment with different solutions to score goals.

9. Seek Feedback:

- Seek feedback from coaches and teammates: Ask for constructive feedback on your decision-making and anticipation skills.

- Listen to their observations and suggestions, implementing them into your training and gameplay.

10. Analyze Top Players:

- Study top players in your position: Analyze how they anticipate and make decisions in the final third.

- Observe their movement, runs, passing decisions, and shooting choices to gain insights into their decision-making processes.

Improving anticipation and decision-making in the final third takes practice, experience, and a deep understanding of the game. By developing your game awareness, timing, and ability to make quick decisions, you can become a more effective and creative attacker, consistently making the right choices to create goal-scoring opportunities.

Chapter 7: Developing a Deadly Instinct in the Box

Reading the game and anticipating scoring opportunities

Reading the game and anticipating scoring opportunities is a crucial skill for attacking players in soccer. By understanding the flow of the game and being able to predict where and when scoring opportunities will arise, you can position yourself strategically and increase your chances of scoring. Here are some techniques to help you improve your ability to read the game and anticipate scoring opportunities:

1. Develop Game Awareness:
   - Maintain a high level of awareness: Continuously scan the field to assess the positioning of defenders, the movement of your teammates, and the spaces available.
   - Be aware of the game situation, including the scoreline, time remaining, and the importance of the match.

2. Study Opponents:
   - Analyze opponents' defensive patterns: Observe how defenders position themselves, mark players, and react to different game situations.
   - Identify weaknesses or vulnerabilities in their defense that you can exploit.

3. Understand Team Tactics:
   - Grasp your team's tactical approach: Understand the playing style and strategies employed by your team.
   - Recognize the patterns of play and the positions your teammates are likely to take up in different phases of the game.

4. Anticipate Passing Options:
   - Predict passing options: Anticipate where your teammates are likely to pass the ball based on their positions and movements.
   - Position yourself in areas where you can receive the ball in a favorable position to create goal-scoring opportunities.

5. Read Defenders' Body Language:
   - Observe defenders' body language: Pay attention to how defenders position themselves and react to different situations.
   - Look for signs of indecision or shifts in weight that may indicate their intention to close down space or commit to a challenge.

6. Analyze Ball Speed and Trajectory:
   - Assess ball speed and trajectory: Judge the speed and trajectory of passes or crosses to anticipate where the ball will end up.
   - This will help you position yourself in the right areas to receive or attack the ball effectively.

7. Study the Goalkeeper:
    - Analyze the goalkeeper's positioning: Observe the goalkeeper's positioning and movement to anticipate potential scoring opportunities.
    - Look for gaps or areas where the goalkeeper might be vulnerable, such as off their line or favoring a particular side of the goal.

8. Visualize Scoring Opportunities:
    - Mentally rehearse scoring opportunities: Visualize different scenarios and how they might unfold.
    - Imagine yourself in scoring positions and think about the movements and decisions you would make to capitalize on those opportunities.

9. Learn from Experience:
    - Reflect on previous matches: Review your performances and identify instances where you successfully anticipated scoring opportunities or missed out on them.
    - Learn from both successful and unsuccessful moments, adjusting your anticipation and decision-making approach accordingly.

10. Play Small-Sided Games and Training Drills:
    - Engage in small-sided games and training drills that simulate game-like situations: These exercises provide opportunities to practice reading the game and anticipating scoring opportunities.

- Work on positioning yourself to receive the ball and make goal-scoring runs based on the movements of your teammates and opponents.

Reading the game and anticipating scoring opportunities takes practice, experience, and a deep understanding of the sport. By enhancing your game awareness, studying opponents, and analyzing the movements of players and the ball, you can improve your ability to read the game effectively and position yourself to take advantage of scoring opportunities when they arise.

Improving reaction time and instinctive finishing

Improving reaction time and instinctive finishing are vital skills for goal-scoring in soccer. These abilities allow you to react quickly to scoring opportunities and make split-second decisions to put the ball in the back of the net. Here are some techniques to help you improve your reaction time and instinctive finishing:

1. Quick Decision-Making Drills:
   - Engage in drills that require rapid decision-making: Set up small-sided games or training exercises that simulate game scenarios with limited time and space.
   - Practice making quick decisions on whether to shoot, pass, or dribble to develop your instinctive decision-making skills.

2. Reaction Training:
   - Incorporate reaction training into your workouts: Use reaction balls, agility ladders, or light cues to enhance your reflexes and response time.
   - Perform exercises that require quick reactions, such as reacting to visual or auditory cues, to improve your ability to respond swiftly in game situations.

3. Visual Focus:
   - Develop a keen visual focus: Keep your eyes on the ball at all times and maintain a wide field of vision.
   - Train yourself to quickly scan the field, identify scoring opportunities, and react accordingly.

4. Practice Repetitions:
   - Practice high-intensity repetitions: Perform shooting drills that require quick reactions and rapid shooting.
   - Repeat these drills frequently to build muscle memory and improve your ability to finish instinctively without hesitation.

5. Anticipate the Play:
   - Anticipate the movements of teammates and opponents: Develop the ability to read the game and anticipate where the ball is going to be played.
   - Position yourself proactively, predicting potential scoring opportunities before they happen.

6. Develop a Feel for the Ball:
   - Enhance your touch and feel for the ball: Spend time practicing ball control exercises to develop a close relationship with the ball.
   - Work on techniques such as juggling, ball manipulation, and quick touches to improve your overall ball handling skills.

7. Visualize Scenarios:
   - Mentally rehearse different game scenarios: Visualize various situations in which you need to react quickly and finish instinctively.
   - Imagine the movements, decisions, and techniques you would employ to convert scoring opportunities into goals.

8. Analyze Top Strikers:
   - Study the techniques of top strikers: Observe how they react to scoring opportunities, their positioning, and their finishing techniques.
   - Analyze their decision-making and note any patterns or strategies that you can incorporate into your own game.

9. Learn from Experience:
   - Reflect on your performances: Review past matches and training sessions to identify instances where your reaction time was effective or needs improvement.
   - Learn from both successful and unsuccessful moments, adjusting your approach and refining your instincts based on those experiences.

10. Play Competitive Matches:
- Engage in competitive matches: Regularly participate in matches against strong opponents to challenge yourself and enhance your ability to react quickly under pressure.
- Competing in a competitive environment will sharpen your instincts and help you make better decisions in goal-scoring situations.

Improving reaction time and instinctive finishing takes practice, focus, and repetition. By incorporating these techniques into your training routine and maintaining a proactive mindset, you can enhance your ability to react quickly and finish instinctively, ultimately becoming a more lethal goal-scorer.

Positioning in the box for tap-ins, headers, and poacher goals

Positioning in the box is crucial for goal-scoring opportunities such as tap-ins, headers, and poacher goals. Proper positioning allows you to be in the right place at the right time to capitalize on chances and increase your goal-scoring efficiency. Here are some tips for positioning in the box for different types of goals:

1. Tap-Ins:
   - Position yourself near the goal line: Move close to the goal line, preferably near the far post, to be in a prime position for tap-ins.
   - Anticipate crosses and cutbacks: Read the movements of your teammates and anticipate when they are likely to deliver a ball into the box.
   - Time your run: Make a late, well-timed run into the box just as the cross is being delivered, giving you the best chance to reach the ball before defenders or the goalkeeper.

2. Headers:
   - Identify the flight of the cross: Assess the trajectory and pace of the cross to anticipate where the ball will arrive.
   - Position yourself between defenders: Look to find gaps or spaces between defenders to provide yourself with the best chance of winning the header.
   - Use your body and timing: Use your body positioning and timing to outmaneuver defenders and get into a strong position to attack the ball with your head.

3. Poacher Goals:
   - Be aware of loose balls and rebounds: Position yourself centrally, within the six-yard box or near the penalty spot, to be ready for any loose balls or rebounds that may occur.
   - React quickly: Stay alert and react immediately when the ball is loose, showing quick reflexes to capitalize on any defensive mistakes or rebounds.

- Stay active and mobile: Constantly move within the box, making small adjustments to position yourself in areas where you can take advantage of any goal-scoring opportunities that arise.

4. Read the game and anticipate:
   - Anticipate crosses and shots: Read the game and anticipate when crosses or shots are likely to be played into the box.
   - Position yourself in areas where you predict the ball will be played based on the movement of your teammates or the attacking phase of play.
   - Stay one step ahead of defenders by positioning yourself in goal-scoring areas before the ball arrives.

5. Communication with teammates:
   - Communicate with your teammates: Use verbal and non-verbal cues to signal your intention to be in a specific position within the box.
   - Coordinate with your teammates to ensure that you are not occupying the same space, maximizing the chances of one of you getting on the end of a scoring opportunity.

6. Study defenders and the goalkeeper:
   - Analyze the defenders' positioning: Observe the positioning and movement of defenders to identify areas where they may leave gaps or fail to track your runs.
   - Pay attention to the goalkeeper's positioning: Note how the goalkeeper positions themselves during

crosses and shots, and adjust your positioning accordingly to exploit any weaknesses or areas they leave open.

7. Learn from experience:
    *   Reflect on previous matches and goals: Review your goals and assess the positions from which you were successful.
    *   Analyze situations where you missed opportunities and determine how you could have positioned yourself better.
    *   Learn from both successful and unsuccessful moments to continuously refine your positioning in the box.

Positioning in the box requires anticipation, awareness, and the ability to read the game. By mastering these techniques and understanding where to position yourself for tap-ins, headers, and poacher goals, you can significantly increase your goal-scoring efficiency and contribute more effectively to your team's success.

Training drills to enhance predatory instincts

To enhance predatory instincts and develop the ability to score goals instinctively, here are some training drills that can help improve your goal-scoring prowess:

1. Finishing from Crosses:
   - Set up a drill with a wide player delivering crosses from the flanks.
   - Position yourself centrally in the box and work on making quick adjustments to get into scoring positions.
   - Focus on reacting instinctively to the flight of the ball and finishing with precision and accuracy.

2. Small-Sided Games:
   - Engage in small-sided games with limited space and quick transitions.
   - Emphasize quick decision-making and instinctive finishing in high-pressure situations.
   - Work on capitalizing on loose balls, rebounds, or any scoring opportunities that arise.

3. Fast Breaks and Counterattacks:
   - Set up scenarios where your team initiates fast breaks or counterattacks against a defense that is recovering.
   - Practice making quick, instinctive runs into goal-scoring positions.
   - Work on finishing with composure and accuracy under pressure.

4. Deflection and Redirect Drills:
   - Create drills that involve deflections or redirection of the ball.
   - Position yourself in the box and work on reacting quickly to redirect the ball towards the goal.

- Focus on adjusting your body position and using deft touches to guide the ball into the net.

5. Reactive Shooting Drills:
   - Set up shooting drills where the ball is played to you from different angles and distances.
   - Focus on reacting quickly to the pass or service and instinctively shooting on target.
   - Incorporate variations such as volleys, one-touch finishes, or quick turns and shots to simulate different game scenarios.

6. Scrimmages with Limited Touches:
   - Play scrimmages where players are limited to one or two touches only.
   - This forces you to make quick decisions and instinctive movements, relying on your predatory instincts to score goals efficiently.

7. Goalmouth Scramble:
   - Set up a scenario where multiple players are vying for a loose ball in the goalmouth area.
   - Practice reacting quickly to the chaos and positioning yourself to finish the ball into the net.
   - Emphasize sharp reflexes and being first to react in goalmouth situations.

8. Visualization Exercises:
   - Incorporate visualization exercises into your training routine.

- Close your eyes and mentally rehearse different scoring scenarios, imagining yourself reacting instinctively and finishing with precision.
- Visualize the movements, decisions, and techniques required to score goals in a variety of situations.

9. Shadow Striker:
   - Play the role of a shadow striker in training sessions.
   - Position yourself between the midfield and defensive lines, making quick, instinctive runs into goal-scoring positions.
   - Focus on timing your movements and being proactive in seeking scoring opportunities.

10. Analysis and Feedback:
    - Review video footage of your matches or training sessions.
    - Analyze your positioning, movement, and decision-making in goal-scoring situations.
    - Seek feedback from coaches and teammates to gain insights into areas for improvement and further hone your predatory instincts.

Developing predatory instincts requires repetition, game awareness, and a willingness to take risks. By incorporating these training drills into your routine and constantly seeking opportunities to react instinctively in goal-scoring situations, you can sharpen your predatory instincts and become a more clinical and opportunistic goal-scorer.

Chapter 8: Mental Strategies for Overcoming Goalkeeper Challenges

Analyzing goalkeepers' weaknesses and exploiting them

Analyzing goalkeepers' weaknesses and exploiting them can be an effective strategy for goal-scoring in soccer. By identifying and targeting specific weaknesses, you can increase your chances of finding the back of the net. Here are some steps to help you analyze goalkeepers' weaknesses and exploit them effectively:

1. Research and Observe:
    *   Study the goalkeeper's previous performances: Watch game footage or review statistical data to identify any recurring patterns or weaknesses.
    *   Pay attention to their positioning, handling of crosses, shot-stopping abilities, distribution, and reactions to different types of shots.

2. Shot Placement:
    *   Analyze the goalkeeper's positioning: Observe whether they tend to favor one side of the goal or leave certain areas more vulnerable.
    *   Look for gaps between the goalkeeper and the near post, or areas where the goalkeeper struggles to cover quickly.
    *   Aim your shots to exploit these areas and increase the chances of scoring.

3. Testing Their Handling:
   - Test the goalkeeper's handling: Shoot with power or place shots in areas where the goalkeeper tends to struggle with collecting or holding onto the ball.
   - Look for situations where the goalkeeper spills rebounds or fails to control shots effectively.
   - Anticipate loose balls and be ready to pounce on any rebounds or mishandled saves to score.

4. Utilize Low Shots and Diving Techniques:
   - Test the goalkeeper's ability to save low shots: Observe whether they struggle with shots close to the ground.
   - Shoot low and with accuracy, aiming for the corners or areas where the goalkeeper may have difficulty reaching.

5. Exploit Weaknesses in Crosses:
   - Analyze the goalkeeper's handling of crosses and high balls: Identify if they struggle with aerial challenges, decision-making, or positioning.
   - Look for situations where the goalkeeper may hesitate or have difficulty coming off their line to claim crosses.
   - Take advantage of these weaknesses by making well-timed runs and attacking high balls aggressively.

6. Quick and Early Shots:
   - Exploit the goalkeeper's reaction time: Observe whether the goalkeeper tends to react slowly to shots.

- Take advantage of quick or early shots, catching the goalkeeper off guard before they have time to set themselves or react.

7. Target Weak Distribution:
   - Analyze the goalkeeper's distribution: Observe if they have any weaknesses in their kicking or throwing abilities.
   - Apply pressure when they have the ball to force them into making errors or making poor decisions with their distribution.
   - Position yourself strategically to intercept or pressurize the goalkeeper's passes and capitalize on any mistakes.

8. Set Pieces:
   - Target the goalkeeper on set pieces: Observe their positioning and how they deal with aerial challenges during corners or free kicks.
   - Position yourself intelligently to exploit any gaps or areas where the goalkeeper may struggle to reach or clear the ball effectively.

9. Learn from Teammates' Experiences:
   - Seek insights from teammates: Discuss with teammates who have previously faced the goalkeeper or have experienced success against them.
   - Share information and strategies to collectively exploit the goalkeeper's weaknesses.

10. Adapt and Adjust:
    - Remain adaptable and observant during the game: Continuously monitor the goalkeeper's positioning, reactions, and any emerging weaknesses throughout the match.
    - Adjust your shooting techniques, runs, and decision-making based on real-time observations to exploit any new vulnerabilities.

Analyzing goalkeepers' weaknesses requires careful observation, game awareness, and adaptability. By identifying their weaknesses and tailoring your shooting techniques and decision-making accordingly, you can increase your effectiveness in scoring goals and become a more successful goal-scorer.

Techniques for outsmarting goalkeepers during one-on-one situations

One-on-one situations with the goalkeeper can be decisive moments in a soccer match. To outsmart goalkeepers and increase your chances of scoring in these situations, consider the following techniques:

1. Eye Contact and Body Language:
    - Establish eye contact with the goalkeeper: Lock eyes with the goalkeeper to create a psychological advantage.

- Use deceptive body language to mislead the goalkeeper about your intended direction or shot placement.
- Keep your body relaxed to maintain an element of surprise and prevent the goalkeeper from reading your intentions.

2. Change of Pace and Direction:
   - Employ changes of pace and direction: Use quick bursts of speed and sudden changes in direction to confuse the goalkeeper.
   - Shift your body weight and direction rapidly to create separation and exploit any gaps in the goalkeeper's positioning.

3. Delayed Shot:
   - Delay your shot: Instead of shooting immediately, delay your shot to force the goalkeeper to commit or make the first move.
   - Watch for the goalkeeper's reactions and choose the optimal moment to strike the ball or take them by surprise with a delayed shot.

4. Use Feints and Dribbling Skills:
   - Incorporate feints and dribbling skills: Utilize feints, such as body feints, stepovers, or fake shots, to deceive the goalkeeper and create openings.
   - Practice various dribbling techniques, including quick changes of direction and close ball control, to maneuver past the goalkeeper.

5. Chip or Lob:
   - Employ chips or lobs: If the goalkeeper rushes out aggressively, consider chipping or lobbing the ball over them.
   - Take advantage of their position and timing by lofting the ball with precision to beat them while they are off their line.

6. Placement and Accuracy:
   - Focus on shot placement: Aim for areas of the goal that are difficult for the goalkeeper to reach.
   - Target the corners or areas where there is less chance of the goalkeeper making a save, such as near the post or just out of their diving range.

7. Body Feints and Shoulder Drops:
   - Utilize body feints and shoulder drops: Use subtle movements of your body and shoulders to deceive the goalkeeper about your intended direction.
   - Use these feints to manipulate the goalkeeper's positioning and create openings for shots or openings to go past them.

8. Quick Releases:
   - Employ quick releases: Shoot early and catch the goalkeeper off guard, before they have time to react or set themselves.
   - Take advantage of any momentary gaps in the goalkeeper's positioning to release your shot rapidly.

9. Off-the-Ball Movement:
    • Make intelligent runs: Time your run into the one-on-one situation to catch the goalkeeper by surprise.
    • Utilize diagonal or curved runs to create separation from defenders and gain a clear path to goal.

10. Practice and Learn from Experience:
    • Regularly practice one-on-one drills: Set up scenarios that replicate one-on-one situations in training.
    • Learn from your experiences in games and training sessions, analyzing what works and what doesn't, and adapt your techniques accordingly.

Outsmarting goalkeepers in one-on-one situations requires a combination of technique, composure, and game awareness. By mastering these techniques and remaining adaptable, you can increase your effectiveness in beating goalkeepers and scoring goals during these critical moments in the game.

Penalty-taking strategies for high success rates

Penalty-taking is a high-pressure situation that requires composure, technique, and strategic decision-making. To increase your success rate in penalty shootouts, consider the following strategies:

1. Stay Calm and Confident:
   - Maintain a calm and confident demeanor: Approach the penalty spot with confidence and a positive mindset.
   - Control your emotions and focus on executing your technique effectively.

2. Pre-shot Routine:
   - Develop a pre-shot routine: Establish a consistent routine that helps you mentally and physically prepare for the penalty.
   - This routine can include steps such as deep breaths, visualizing success, or a specific approach to the ball.

3. Research and Analyze the Goalkeeper:
   - Study the goalkeeper: Research the goalkeeper's penalty-saving tendencies and preferences.
   - Observe if they tend to dive early, favor a particular side, or have a specific technique for saving penalties.
   - Use this information to inform your shot placement and decision-making.

4. Shot Placement and Accuracy:
   - Aim for the corners: Focus on placing your shot in the corners of the goal.
   - The corners are harder for the goalkeeper to reach, increasing the chances of scoring.
   - Aim for the side that you feel most comfortable with or based on your analysis of the goalkeeper's tendencies.

5. Change of Speed and Technique:
   - Incorporate changes of speed and technique: Vary your shot technique and speed to keep the goalkeeper guessing.
   - Consider mixing up your penalties with fast, powerful shots and slower, placement-based shots to add unpredictability.

6. Deception and Feints:
   - Use deception and feints: Employ subtle feints or changes in body language to deceive the goalkeeper.
   - Use your eyes, body positioning, or shooting motion to create uncertainty for the goalkeeper before taking the shot.

7. Practice Under Pressure:
   - Simulate pressure in practice: Replicate high-pressure penalty situations during training.
   - Practice penalties with teammates or in penalty shootout simulations to enhance your ability to perform under pressure.

8. Mental Visualization:
   - Visualize success: Spend time visualizing successful penalty kicks and imagine yourself executing the perfect shot.
   - Visualization can help build confidence and reinforce positive outcomes in your mind.

9. Learn from Previous Penalties:
    - Reflect on previous penalties: Analyze your past penalty kicks and identify any patterns or areas for improvement.
    - Learn from your experiences and adjust your technique and decision-making based on what has worked well or needs refinement.

10. Develop Penalty-Specific Skills:
    - Focus on penalty-specific skills: Dedicate training time to develop penalty-taking skills, including shot placement, power, and accuracy.
    - Practice penalties regularly to build muscle memory and develop confidence in your technique.

Penalty shootouts are as much a mental battle as they are a technical one. By employing these strategies, practicing consistently, and maintaining composure, you can increase your success rate and become a reliable penalty taker for your team.

Maintaining composure in front of the goal

Maintaining composure in front of the goal is essential for converting goal-scoring opportunities with accuracy and consistency. Here are some techniques to help you stay composed in crucial moments:

1. Focus on Technique:
    *   Concentrate on your technique: Trust in the skills and techniques you have practiced.
    *   Focus on executing your technique properly, whether it's shooting, passing, or dribbling, without allowing external factors to distract you.

2. Controlled Breathing:
    *   Practice controlled breathing: Take deep breaths to help regulate your heart rate and calm your nerves.
    *   Inhale deeply through your nose, hold for a second, and exhale slowly through your mouth.
    *   Controlled breathing can help reduce anxiety and maintain composure.

3. Positive Self-Talk:
    *   Use positive self-talk: Encourage yourself with positive and affirming statements.
    *   Repeat phrases like "I can do this," "I am confident," or "I will make the right decision."
    *   Replace any negative or self-doubting thoughts with positive affirmations.

4. Visualize Success:
   - Visualize successful outcomes: Imagine yourself executing the desired action with precision and success.
   - Visualize scoring goals, making accurate passes, or beating the goalkeeper with confidence.
   - This mental imagery reinforces positive expectations and helps you maintain composure.

5. Stay Present:
   - Focus on the present moment: Avoid dwelling on past missed opportunities or worrying about future outcomes.
   - Stay fully present in the current situation, focusing on the task at hand.
   - Clear your mind of distractions and focus on the immediate goal-scoring opportunity.

6. Manage Time Pressure:
   - Develop a sense of time: Be aware of the time available to make decisions and execute your actions.
   - Avoid rushing or panicking by recognizing that you have the necessary time to make the right choice.
   - This awareness will help you stay composed and make better decisions.

7. Control Body Language:
   - Display confident body language: Stand tall, maintain an upright posture, and keep your body relaxed.
   - Project confidence through your body language, even if you may feel nervous internally.

- Positive body language can contribute to a composed and confident mindset.

8. Stick to Your Game Plan:
   - Stick to your game plan: Focus on the strategies and tactics that have been practiced and implemented.
   - Trust the game plan developed by your team and coaches, knowing that it is designed for success.
   - This confidence in your team's preparation can help you maintain composure.

9. Experience and Learn:
   - Draw from past experiences: Recall moments when you remained composed and performed well under pressure.
   - Reflect on those instances and remind yourself that you have the capability to maintain composure and succeed.

10. Practice Under Pressure:
    - Simulate pressure situations in practice: Create drills and scenarios that replicate high-pressure game situations.
    - Practice maintaining composure while executing game-like actions, such as shooting or making decisions in tight spaces.
    - Regular exposure to pressure situations in training will help you build composure over time.

Remember, maintaining composure is a skill that can be developed with practice and mental discipline. By incorporating these techniques into your training and mental preparation, you can improve your ability to stay composed in front of the goal and maximize your goal-scoring potential.

Chapter 9: Training Regimens for Goal-Scorers

Tailoring practice sessions to improve shooting and finishing skills

To improve shooting and finishing skills, it's important to tailor your practice sessions specifically to target these areas. Here are some tips for designing practice sessions focused on shooting and finishing:

1. Set Clear Objectives:
   - Define specific objectives for each practice session: Identify the particular shooting and finishing skills you want to work on, such as accuracy, power, technique, or different types of finishes.
   - Having clear objectives helps you structure your practice and measure your progress over time.

2. Repetition and Consistency:
   - Incorporate repetition into your practice: Repeatedly perform shooting and finishing drills to reinforce muscle memory and develop a consistent technique.
   - Consistency in practice helps transfer the skills into game situations.

3. Varied Shooting Scenarios:
   - Create a variety of shooting scenarios: Design drills that simulate different game situations, such as shooting from different angles, distances, and body positions.

- Include shooting from crosses, through balls, set pieces, and dribbling scenarios to replicate real game scenarios.

4. Technique Development:
   - Focus on proper shooting technique: Devote time to refining your shooting technique, including body positioning, balance, follow-through, and striking the ball cleanly.
   - Work on specific elements such as using different parts of your foot (laces, instep), volleys, chips, and headers to develop a diverse skill set.

5. Targeted Accuracy and Placement:
   - Practice shooting with accuracy and placement: Incorporate target-based drills to improve your ability to place shots precisely.
   - Set up targets or designated areas within the goal to aim for, helping you develop the skill to hit specific spots consistently.

6. Game-like Pressure:
   - Simulate game-like pressure situations: Introduce pressure elements into your practice to simulate real-game conditions.
   - For example, have defenders apply light pressure or time your shots to create a sense of urgency, forcing you to make quick decisions and shoot accurately.

7. Incorporate Decision-Making:
   - Integrate decision-making into shooting drills: Include scenarios that require you to make quick decisions on whether to shoot, pass, or dribble.
   - Practice identifying the optimal moment to shoot based on the positioning of defenders, the goalkeeper, and your teammates.

8. Feedback and Analysis:
   - Seek feedback from coaches or training partners: Request feedback on your shooting technique, accuracy, and decision-making.
   - Analyze your performance, identify areas for improvement, and make adjustments accordingly.

9. Video Analysis:
   - Use video analysis: Record your practice sessions or games and review the footage to analyze your shooting and finishing technique.
   - Look for areas where you can make improvements, identify strengths, and learn from successful goal-scoring moments.

10. Game Simulation:
    - Incorporate shooting and finishing into small-sided games: Engage in small-sided games that provide opportunities to practice shooting and finishing within a game context.
    - Apply the skills you have developed during practice and focus on replicating your techniques and decision-making under game-like conditions.

Consistency, repetition, and targeted practice are key to improving shooting and finishing skills. By designing practice sessions that focus specifically on these areas and incorporating game-like elements, you can enhance your goal-scoring abilities and become a more effective finisher on the field.

Incorporating individual and team drills into training routines

Incorporating both individual and team drills into your training routines is essential for well-rounded development as a soccer player. Individual drills help improve specific skills and techniques, while team drills foster collaboration, communication, and understanding of the game's collective aspects. Here are some suggestions for incorporating individual and team drills into your training routine:

Individual Drills:

1. Dribbling Circuit:
    - Set up a circuit with cones or markers where you work on various dribbling techniques, including close control, changes of direction, and speed dribbling.
    - Challenge yourself with different variations such as dribbling through tight spaces or dribbling at high speeds.

2. Shooting Accuracy:
   - Practice shooting accuracy by setting up targets or using target nets.
   - Work on striking the ball accurately and consistently, aiming for specific areas of the goal.

3. Passing and Receiving:
   - Set up passing and receiving drills that focus on improving your technique, first touch, and accuracy.
   - Include different types of passes such as short passes, long passes, and through balls to develop a well-rounded passing game.

4. Speed and Agility:
   - Incorporate speed and agility drills into your routine to enhance your quickness and explosiveness.
   - Use ladder drills, cone drills, or shuttle runs to improve your footwork, agility, and overall speed on the field.

5. Individual Decision-Making:
   - Practice decision-making in game-like scenarios where you have to make quick choices on whether to pass, dribble, or shoot.
   - Use cones or teammates as defenders to create pressure and simulate real-game situations.

Team Drills:

1. Possession Drills:
   - Engage in possession-based drills that emphasize maintaining control of the ball as a team.
   - Focus on passing accuracy, off-the-ball movement, and quick decision-making to keep possession in tight spaces.

2. Small-Sided Games:
   - Play small-sided games that encourage teamwork, communication, and the application of individual skills in a collective setting.
   - Emphasize specific objectives, such as playing out from the back, creating scoring opportunities, or working on defensive organization.

3. Tactical Drills:
   - Incorporate tactical drills that focus on team formations, defensive shape, attacking patterns, and set-piece plays.
   - Work on understanding your role within the team structure and executing specific tactical instructions.

4. Combination Play:
   - Practice combination plays that involve coordinated movements, passing sequences, and overlapping runs.
   - Emphasize the importance of timing, communication, and understanding your teammates' tendencies.

5. Game Simulation:
   - Simulate game scenarios during training sessions, such as 11 vs. 11 matches or specific game situations like counterattacks or transitions.
   - Apply the skills and techniques you've developed in individual drills within a team context.

6. Set-Piece Training:
   - Allocate time for set-piece training, including offensive and defensive corner kicks, free kicks, and penalty kicks.
   - Work on coordination, positioning, and execution of set-piece strategies as a team.

7. Communication and Team Bonding:
   - Promote communication and team bonding activities within your training sessions.
   - Encourage open communication, positive reinforcement, and unity to foster better teamwork on and off the field.

A well-rounded training routine incorporates both individual and team drills. Balancing individual skill development with team dynamics and understanding is crucial for overall improvement as a soccer player. By dedicating time to both types of drills, you can enhance your individual abilities while also contributing effectively to the success of your team.

Physical conditioning for explosive shooting and sustained performance

Physical conditioning plays a vital role in developing explosive shooting power and sustaining performance throughout a soccer match. Here are some key aspects of physical conditioning that can enhance your shooting abilities and overall performance:

1. Cardiovascular Endurance:
   - Develop cardiovascular endurance through activities like running, interval training, or high-intensity interval training (HIIT).
   - Improved cardiovascular fitness allows you to sustain high-intensity efforts for longer periods, ensuring consistent performance throughout the match.

2. Strength Training:
   - Engage in strength training exercises targeting the lower body, core, and upper body to improve overall strength and power.
   - Focus on exercises such as squats, lunges, deadlifts, plyometrics, and medicine ball exercises to develop explosive leg power for shooting.

3. Plyometric Training:
   - Incorporate plyometric exercises to enhance explosiveness and power in your shooting.
   - Exercises like box jumps, bounding, and depth jumps help improve muscle elasticity, fast-twitch muscle fiber recruitment, and power generation.

4. Agility and Quickness:
   - Practice agility and quickness drills to improve your ability to change direction rapidly and react quickly in shooting situations.
   - Cone drills, ladder drills, and shuttle runs can enhance your footwork, agility, and speed of movement.

5. Core Stability:
   - Strengthen your core muscles to enhance stability and generate power in your shooting technique.
   - Exercises like planks, Russian twists, and medicine ball rotational throws help improve core strength and stability.

6. Flexibility and Mobility:
   - Incorporate stretching and mobility exercises into your routine to maintain flexibility and range of motion.
   - Dynamic stretching and mobility drills prepare your muscles for explosive movements and help prevent injuries.

7. High-Intensity Interval Training (HIIT):
   - Incorporate HIIT workouts into your training routine to simulate the intensity of match situations.
   - Interval training involving short bursts of high-intensity exercise followed by active recovery periods helps improve your ability to perform explosive efforts repeatedly.

8. Speed and Sprint Training:
   - Include speed and sprint training sessions to develop acceleration and top-end speed.
   - Perform interval sprints, hill sprints, or shuttle runs to enhance your speed, quickness, and explosive power.

9. Endurance Training:
   - Incorporate longer distance running or aerobic exercises to build endurance and improve your ability to sustain performance over the course of a match.
   - This type of training helps you maintain energy levels and focus during extended periods of play.

10. Recovery and Rest:
    - Allow sufficient time for recovery and rest between training sessions and matches.
    - Adequate sleep, proper nutrition, and active recovery techniques like foam rolling or stretching aid in muscle repair and help prevent fatigue and overuse injuries.

A comprehensive physical conditioning program should be tailored to your specific needs and consider your position on the field. Consult with a qualified strength and conditioning coach to design a program that suits your goals and helps maximize your shooting power and sustained performance on the pitch.

Assessing progress and tracking improvement over time

Assessing your progress and tracking improvement over time is crucial for monitoring your development as a soccer player. Here are some effective ways to assess progress and track improvement:

1. Goal Setting:
   - Set specific, measurable, achievable, relevant, and time-bound (SMART) goals for your soccer skills and performance.
   - Regularly review and assess your progress toward these goals to determine your improvement over time.

2. Performance Metrics:
   - Track and record relevant performance metrics, such as goals scored, assists, shooting accuracy, passing completion rate, or distance covered during matches.
   - Compare these metrics over time to identify trends and improvements in specific areas of your game.

3. Game Evaluation:
   - Reflect on your performance after matches and training sessions.
   - Assess your strengths and weaknesses, identifying areas that require improvement.
   - Take note of any changes in your decision-making, technique, positioning, or overall impact on the game.

4. Video Analysis:
   - Record and review your matches or training sessions using video analysis tools.
   - Analyze your performance to identify areas for improvement in your technique, movement, positioning, and decision-making.
   - Compare your current performances with past recordings to assess progress and identify areas of growth.

5. Skill Assessments:
   - Conduct periodic skill assessments to evaluate your proficiency in specific soccer skills, such as shooting, passing, dribbling, or defensive techniques.
   - Use standardized tests or drills to measure your performance and track improvement over time.

6. Training Evaluation:
   - Assess the effectiveness of your training sessions and programs.
   - Evaluate the quality and intensity of your practice sessions, as well as the progression of exercises and drills.
   - Consider feedback from coaches or trainers to gauge your improvement in areas targeted during training.

7. Physical Fitness Testing:
   - Conduct regular physical fitness tests to assess your overall fitness levels.

- Measure components such as speed, agility, strength, power, and endurance to track improvements in your physical conditioning.

8. Coach and Peer Feedback:
   - Seek feedback from your coach, trainers, and teammates on your performance.
   - Actively listen to their observations and suggestions for improvement.
   - Regular feedback sessions provide valuable insights and help you assess your progress from an external perspective.

9. Competition and Performance:
   - Evaluate your performance in competitive matches against different opponents.
   - Assess your ability to execute specific skills, make effective decisions, and contribute to your team's success.
   - Take note of any changes in your effectiveness and impact on the game.

10. Self-Assessment:
    - Engage in regular self-assessment by critically reflecting on your development.
    - Identify areas where you have made progress and areas that still require improvement.
    - Celebrate your successes and use your self-assessment as motivation to continue working on areas of growth.

By consistently assessing your progress and tracking improvement over time, you can identify areas for development, set new goals, and adjust your training and practice routines accordingly. Remember to maintain a growth mindset and view each assessment as an opportunity for growth and learning as you strive to become a better soccer player.

Conclusion:

Recap of key points discussed throughout the book

Throughout the book "Goal-Scoring Artistry: Skill Development and Technique for Deadly Shooting and Finishing in Soccer," we have covered various key points related to improving goal-scoring abilities. Here is a recap of the main topics discussed:

1. Importance of Scoring Goals: Emphasized the significance of goal-scoring in soccer and its impact on team success.
2. Objective of the Book: The book aims to provide comprehensive guidance on skill development and technique for effective shooting and finishing.
3. Understanding the Psychology: Discussed the psychological aspects of goal-scoring, including confidence, focus, mental resilience, visualization, and goal-setting techniques.
4. Perfecting Shooting Technique: Explored the importance of body positioning, balance, and striking the ball cleanly for effective shooting.
5. Footwork for Power and Accuracy: Highlighted the role of footwork in generating power and accuracy in shots.
6. Different Shooting Techniques: Explored various shooting techniques, including laces, instep, volleys, and chips, and when to use each technique.
7. Developing the Weak Foot: Discussed the significance of developing the weak foot for shooting and provided exercises to improve weak foot proficiency.

8. Importance of Accuracy in Finishing: Explored the significance of accuracy in finishing and techniques to improve placement in different areas of the goal.

9. Shooting Drills for Accuracy: Provided a range of shooting drills and exercises specifically designed to enhance accuracy.

10. Shooting under Pressure: Shared tips and strategies to maintain composure and perform well when shooting under pressure situations.

11. Generating Power through Technique: Discussed the importance of proper technique and body mechanics to generate power in shots.

12. Exercises for Leg Strength and Explosive Shooting: Provided specific exercises and drills to develop leg strength and enhance explosive shooting abilities.

13. Shooting from Distance and Outside the Box: Explored techniques for shooting from long range and outside the penalty area.

14. Shooting with Power and Accuracy: Discussed techniques to strike powerful shots while maintaining accuracy and control.

15. Finishing One-on-One with the Goalkeeper: Provided tips and techniques for outsmarting goalkeepers and finishing successfully in one-on-one situations.

16. Understanding Angles and Positions for Finishing: Explored different angles and positions for finishing to maximize goal-scoring opportunities.

17. Shooting in Tight Spaces and Crowded Defenses: Discussed techniques for shooting under pressure in confined spaces and against crowded defenses.

18. Capitalizing on Rebounds and Loose Balls: Explored strategies to seize scoring opportunities from rebounds and loose balls in and around the goalmouth.
19. Creating Space and Intelligent Runs: Discussed the importance of creating space and making intelligent runs to get into goal-scoring positions.
20. Timing Runs and Exploiting Defensive Vulnerabilities: Highlighted the significance of timing runs to stay onside and exploit defensive weaknesses.
21. Analyzing Goal-Scoring Movements: Explored the goal-scoring movements of top strikers for inspiration and learning.
22. Improving Anticipation and Decision-Making: Discussed techniques to enhance anticipation and decision-making skills in the final third.
23. Reading the Game and Anticipating Scoring Opportunities: Explored strategies to read the game effectively and anticipate scoring opportunities.
24. Improving Reaction Time and Instinctive Finishing: Discussed techniques and drills to improve reaction time and develop instinctive finishing abilities.
25. Positioning for Tap-Ins, Headers, and Poacher Goals: Explored the role of positioning in the box for scoring tap-ins, headers, and poacher goals.
26. Training Drills for Predatory Instincts: Provided specific training drills to develop predatory instincts and enhance goal-scoring abilities.
27. Placing Shots in Different Areas of the Goal: Discussed techniques and strategies for placing shots accurately in different areas of the goal.

28. Shooting Drills to Improve Accuracy: Provided a variety of shooting drills and exercises designed to improve accuracy.
29. Tips for Shooting under Pressure: Shared tips and techniques to remain composed and execute accurate shots when under pressure.
30. Generating Power through Technique and Body Mechanics: Discussed the importance of technique and body mechanics in generating power for shooting.
31. Exercises for Leg Strength and Explosive Shooting: Provided exercises and drills to develop leg strength and enhance explosive shooting abilities.
32. Shooting Techniques from Distance and Outside the Box: Explored techniques for shooting with power and accuracy from distance and outside the box.
33. Techniques for Finishing One-on-One with the Goalkeeper: Provided tips and techniques to outsmart goalkeepers and finish successfully in one-on-one situations.
34. Understanding Different Angles and Positions for Finishing: Explored the significance of angles and positions for finishing to maximize goal-scoring opportunities.
35. Shooting under Pressure from Tight Spaces and Crowded Defenses: Discussed techniques for shooting accurately and effectively in tight spaces and against crowded defenses.
36. Capitalizing on Rebounds and Loose Balls: Explored strategies to capitalize on rebounds and loose balls in goal-scoring situations.

37. Creating Space and Making Intelligent Runs: Highlighted the importance of creating space and making intelligent runs to get into goal-scoring positions.
38. Timing Runs and Exploiting Defensive Vulnerabilities: Discussed techniques for timing runs to stay onside and exploit defensive vulnerabilities.
39. Analyzing Goalkeepers' Weaknesses and Exploiting Them: Explored techniques to assess goalkeepers' weaknesses and exploit them to increase scoring chances.
40. Developing Confidence, Focus, and Mental Resilience: Discussed strategies to develop confidence, focus, and mental resilience for improved performance.
41. Visualization and Goal-Setting Techniques: Explored the benefits of visualization and goal-setting techniques to enhance goal-scoring abilities.
42. Individual and Team Drills in Training Routines: Discussed the importance of incorporating both individual and team drills in training routines for comprehensive development.
43. Physical Conditioning for Explosive Shooting and Sustained Performance: Explored the significance of physical conditioning and provided guidance on cardio endurance, strength training, agility, and rest.
44. Assessing Progress and Tracking Improvement over Time: Discussed various methods to assess progress and track improvement, including goal setting, performance metrics, video analysis, and self-assessment.

By revisiting and applying the concepts covered throughout the book, you can enhance your goal-scoring artistry, improve your shooting and finishing abilities, and become a more effective and deadly striker on the soccer field.

Encouragement to continue honing goal-scoring skills through dedicated practice

As you continue on your journey to hone your goal-scoring skills, remember that dedication and consistent practice are the keys to unlocking your true potential. It's essential to remain motivated, inspired, and committed to improving your abilities. Here's some encouragement to keep you going:

1. Embrace the Process: Becoming a skilled goal-scorer is a journey that takes time and effort. Embrace the process of improvement and enjoy every step along the way. Each practice session and training opportunity is an opportunity for growth.

2. Set Ambitious Goals: Challenge yourself by setting ambitious yet achievable goals. Whether it's scoring a certain number of goals in a season, improving your shooting accuracy, or becoming more effective in one-on-one situations, setting specific targets will give you direction and motivation.

3. Celebrate Small Victories: Recognize and celebrate your progress, no matter how small. Each improvement, no matter how incremental, brings you closer to becoming the best version of yourself as a goal-scorer. Take pride in the milestones you achieve along the way.

4. Seek Inspiration: Surround yourself with inspiration from the game. Watch videos of great goal-scorers, study their techniques, and learn from their success stories. Let their accomplishments fuel your desire to excel and inspire you to push beyond your limits.

5. Learn from Setbacks: Understand that setbacks and failures are part of the learning process. Don't be discouraged by missed chances or unsuccessful attempts. Instead, view them as opportunities to learn, adapt, and grow. Analyze what went wrong, make adjustments, and come back stronger.

6. Embrace Feedback: Embrace feedback from coaches, teammates, and mentors. Their insights and guidance can provide valuable perspectives and help you identify areas for improvement. Use constructive criticism as a tool for growth and learning.

7. Practice with Purpose: Every training session is an opportunity to refine your skills. Practice with intention, focusing on the specific aspects of goal-scoring you want to improve. Pay attention to your technique, decision-making, and overall game understanding. Consistent, purposeful practice will yield significant results.

8. Stay Disciplined: Consistency is key to progress. Stay disciplined in your training routine and make goal-scoring practice a regular part of your schedule. Even on days when motivation may waver, rely on discipline to push through and keep moving forward.

9. Stay Positive: Maintain a positive mindset throughout your journey. Believe in your abilities and have confidence in your potential as a goal-scorer. Positive thinking can enhance your performance, boost your motivation, and help you overcome challenges.

10. Enjoy the Journey: Remember to have fun and enjoy the process. Playing and improving your goal-scoring skills should bring you joy and fulfillment. Embrace the passion for the game and relish the moments of success, growth, and camaraderie with your teammates.

By dedicating yourself to continuous practice and improvement, you are investing in your development as a goal-scoring artist. Keep pushing your boundaries, embrace the challenges, and never stop honing your skills. Your hard work and perseverance will pay off, and your goal-scoring prowess will shine on the soccer field.

Inspiring anecdotes and quotes from successful goal-scorers

1. "Every strike brings me closer to the next home run." - Babe Ruth
2. "I've missed more than 9,000 shots in my career. I've lost almost 300 games. Twenty-six times, I've been trusted to take the game-winning shot and missed. I've failed over and over and over again in my life. And that is why I succeed." - Michael Jordan
3. "Success is no accident. It is hard work, perseverance, learning, studying, sacrifice, and most of all, love of what you are doing or learning to do." - Pelé
4. "I've always believed that if you put in the work, the results will come." - Lionel Messi
5. "There may be people who have more talent than you, but there's no excuse for anyone to work harder than you do." - Derek Jeter
6. "You miss 100% of the shots you don't take." - Wayne Gretzky
7. "The greatest glory in living lies not in never falling, but in rising every time we fall." - Nelson Mandela
8. "I don't count my goals; I only count the ones that helped us win." - Mia Hamm
9. "The harder the battle, the sweeter the victory." - Cristiano Ronaldo
10. "It's not about the shoes, it's about what you do in them." - Michael Jordan
11. "You have to fight to reach your dream. You have to sacrifice and work hard for it." - Zlatan Ibrahimović

12. "Success is no accident. It's hard work, perseverance, learning, studying, sacrifice, and most of all, love of what you are doing." - Cristiano Ronaldo
13. "When you've got something to prove, there's nothing greater than a challenge." - Cristiano Ronaldo
14. "I've always said I wanted to be remembered as a player who didn't waste a moment, who tried to be a winner in every game, and who tried to give everything to his team." - Francesco Totti
15. "There's no secret formula. I lift heavy, work hard, and aim to be the best." - Alex Morgan

These anecdotes and quotes from successful goal-scorers remind us of the dedication, hard work, and determination required to excel in the art of scoring goals. They inspire us to push through challenges, embrace failure as an opportunity for growth, and strive for greatness in our own goal-scoring endeavors.

Final thoughts on the artistry and joy of scoring goals in soccer

The artistry and joy of scoring goals in soccer are unparalleled. It is a culmination of skill, technique, creativity, and instinct coming together in a moment of pure elation. As a goal-scorer, you have the unique ability to leave an indelible mark on the game and bring immeasurable joy to yourself and your team.

Scoring a goal is not just about putting the ball into the back of the net. It is an expression of your passion, determination, and dedication to the sport. It is a testament to the countless hours spent practicing, refining your technique, and honing your skills. It is a reflection of your ability to read the game, make split-second decisions, and execute with precision.

The artistry of scoring goals lies in the creativity and flair you bring to your finishes. Whether it's a powerful strike from distance, a delicate chip over the goalkeeper, a perfectly placed header, or a skillful dribble past defenders, each goal is a unique masterpiece created by your imagination and execution.

But beyond the technical aspects, the joy of scoring goals is what truly makes it special. The rush of adrenaline as the ball finds the back of the net, the roar of the crowd, the jubilant celebrations with your teammates—it's an experience that is unmatched in the world of sports.

Scoring goals not only brings personal satisfaction but also ignites a spark within your team. Your ability to find the back of the net can lift the spirits of your teammates, inspire them to raise their performance, and fuel a winning mentality. It creates a bond, a shared joy, and a sense of accomplishment that unites the team in pursuit of victory.

Remember, the artistry and joy of scoring goals extend beyond individual success. It is about the collective effort, the synergy between teammates, and the shared pursuit of excellence. It is about bringing joy to yourself, your team, and the fans who support you.

So, embrace the artistry of scoring goals, nurture your skills, and revel in the joy that each successful finish brings. Let the passion for the game guide you, and always remember that the true beauty lies not just in the act of scoring but in the journey of growth and the memories you create along the way. Embrace the art, feel the joy, and continue to be a relentless goal-scoring artist on the soccer field.

Printed in Great Britain
by Amazon

42728074R00086